T0160404

PINTS
Minnesota's

NORTH

Craft Beer Culture

Katelyn Regenscheid · Foreword by Doug Hoverson

MINNESOTA HISTORICAL SOCIETY PRESS

mnhspress.org

The Minnesota Historical Society Press
is a member of the Association of University Presses.

Manufactured in the United States of America

10 9 8 7 6 5 4 3 2 1

∞ The paper used in this publication meets the minimum requirements of the American National Standard for Information Sciences—Permanence for Printed Library Materials, ANSI Z39.48-1984.

International Standard Book Number
ISBN: 978-1-68134-170-5 (paper)

Library of Congress Control Number: 2020943821

On the front cover: Beers at Ursa Minor Brewing, Duluth.
On the title pages: Taproom at Bad Weather Brewing Company, St. Paul.
Page vi: Waldmann Brewery, St. Paul.

CONTENTS

FOREWORD

Before you travel with Katelyn Regenscheid through the taprooms of Minnesota, allow me to divert you briefly with a detour through time—to about 150 years ago. The 1860s and 1870s offer the closest comparisons to the recent explosion of small breweries happening in Minnesota and around the country.

Many elements of the post-Civil War Minnesota beer scene would be familiar to an observer of our current world of craft beer. The majority of beer was produced by a few businesses with regional or national aspirations, but the majority of breweries served strictly local markets. Prior to the late 1870s, most beer was served on draught except for a very few bottled ales shipped from cities in the east.

As we hunt around the city looking for the best place to have a beer or two, most of the places serving our prey will be family-owned saloons or hotel bars (sometimes called "sample rooms"). Cities with a significant German culture will have a few beer gardens. But our quest ends when we find the freshest beer in town—at the local brewery.

Stepping inside the brewery's saloon, our senses would be struck by the different atmosphere and culture compared to what we know today. Even before crossing the threshold, we would be conscious of the smoky interior as well as the aroma of tobacco juice rising from spittoons or the floor. Ornate tap handles are nowhere to be found (tap markers featuring the brand name were not required until after Prohibition). We won't see many beer signs on the wall—these didn't become common until the late 1870s—but there may be other art to add some character. There will be no sign of the brewing equipment; it is probably in an entirely separate building.

As we jostle our way to the bar, we notice the assembled crowd is predominantly or exclusively male. The patrons all either live or work in the immediate neighborhood. No "beer travelers" here, other than maybe a traveling salesman or two, or a farmer picking up spent grain from the brewery to use as livestock feed. If we are lucky enough to find a brewery with a beer garden, it will feature that spirit of community and conviviality captured in the German word *gemütlichkeit.* Families are welcome, sharing long tables is essential, and joining in song is expected.

What shall we order? That decision was made the moment we walked in the door or through the gate. While a hotel bar might have a few brands available, often including an out-of-town beer (typically from Milwaukee), the brewery saloon will offer only its own draught beer. As bottled beer became more widely available at the end of the 1870s, large and midsize breweries usually offered from two to five bottled varieties and one or two draught beers. Nearly all of these were variations on the lager theme: Münchner, Wiener, Kulmbacher, and Pilsener. A few German brewers might offer a bottled porter. If we are lucky enough to stumble across Adam Stenger's City Brewery in Rochester or Edward Drewry's brewery in St. Paul, we might have a chance to sample an India pale ale, a stock ale, or a Scotch ale—but these were rare exceptions.

To decompress from our visit to the nineteenth century, let's stop in briefly for refreshment at a brewery hospitality room around 1960. The smoke will still be there, but the spittoons are gone. These hospitality rooms are a place for employees to gather after their shift, for local groups and civic organizations to meet, and for free beer for the lucky friends who can wangle a guest card. State law dictates that breweries may not sell beer directly to consumers, so all the beer will be free. And when we say the beer, we mean *the* beer. You might be able to get a bock in season, or perhaps a specialty such as Hamm's Waldech, but the pitchers will be full of a single flagship beer.

Arriving back in current times, Katelyn Regenscheid now will show us around the taprooms displaying the diversity of modern craft beer. The atmosphere is clearer because of the lack of smoke, so we'll be able to see bars made of materials ranging from stainless steel to repurposed wood. The gender balance of the guests will be much closer to even. Depending on the taproom, children may be playing board games with their parents or romping with the furry friends visiting the many dog-friendly businesses. There won't be as much singing, but song titles may come up during the weekly trivia contests. What to order? Many taprooms have more beer styles on tap at any given time than could be found in the entire state 150 years ago.

Most of us have had the opportunity to be the local guide for the traveler in the seat next to us—and the visitor seeking advice on what to order and what else to see in town. Either way, friendly and interesting conversation is easy to find. Katelyn has learned about taprooms from being an explorer, a regular, and an employee. She has learned how to see our modern beer-drinking experience from a number of angles and has a good sense of how the parts fit together. She asks good questions and listens thoughtfully to the answers. I've enjoyed the chance to have a beer with her and talk about where the brewery taproom has been and where it's going. While she considers the origins of these breweries, the history is important for the stories it creates about each business. These stories, and the type of people attracted to them, give each taproom a different culture. After reading Katelyn's book, you'll see things in your favorite taproom in a broader context. Whether you're drinking your favorite pilsner, imperial stout, or milkshake IPA, let the story behind it all enhance your enjoyment.

Ein Prosit!

Doug Hoverson,
author of *Land of Amber Waters: The History of Brewing in Minnesota*

PREFACE

I was born into craft beer. When the so-called taproom bill passed in May of 2011, I was two months shy of my eighteenth birthday. By the time I turned twenty-one, thirty-five new taprooms had opened in the state in addition to the previously existing production breweries and brewpubs, which were already allowed by state law.

When I came of legal drinking age the summer before my senior year of college, I was drinking beer in a culture that celebrated and continues to celebrate craft. Just months after my twenty-first birthday, I walked up to the bar at the Contented Cow, a pub in my college town of Northfield. Odell's Tree Shaker IPA stuck out on the handwritten chalkboard menu with a tasting note of grapefruit, so I gave it a try, and I was hooked.

At the time, I wasn't self-aware enough to know I was a tiny part of an exploding industry. To be frank, I wasn't self-aware about many things. But I knew enough to recognize something special about this brand-new-to-me phenomenon that was becoming brand new to many other Minnesotans as well. Little did I know how much craft beer would come to mean to me.

In my first professional interactions with the beer industry, I was an intern for a small marketing agency that worked with new breweries as well as established wholesale beer distributors. The internship, which eventually turned into a full-time job, introduced me to a killer culture of local talent, easygoing attitudes, and a damn good product. The people I encountered were motivated entrepreneurs, dedicated purveyors of craft, and pleasantly chill drinking companions.

A few months after starting at that agency, I graduated college and entered the abyss of the real world and suffered from a bit of culture

Fresh hop cones decorate a pint of Inbound BrewCo's Fresh Fruit, a fresh-hopped IPA. Hops are one of the four core ingredients in beer (along with water, yeast, and malted barley or other grain). While most beers incorporate hops in pelletized form, fresh, full cones can be used to impart fresher hop flavors.

shock. No longer were my days filled with reading novels in the quad and studying psychology textbooks. Instead, I was supposed to build a career and mingle at networking events. I continued to work with talented clients in beer as well as several other industries while sleeping in my old bedroom at my parents' house—caught in a limbo between my youth and whatever the hell lay ahead of me.

It was during that purgatory that I decided to undertake a personal project to fill the void: I would visit every taproom in Minnesota. Much like a cross-country road trip in a coming-of-age movie, my endeavor would lead me to new places while teaching me about myself along the way. However, the soundtrack probably involved far more of the Chicks than you hear in the movies. The project started in 2016 and became a years-long journey. Like a good millennial, I chronicled my experiences through a blog—featuring photos and tidbits of life advice I solicited from bartenders, brewers, owners, and a few fellow drinkers after I was a couple beers deep. With my interest piqued by professional experiences and a desire for a postgraduate purpose, it only felt right to dive fully into the beer industry firsthand.

In two years, I drove to, camped near, indulged at, and learned from every one of the 148 open and operating taprooms in Minnesota at the time. One week, I traveled from the far northwest corner of the state in Hallock—near the Canadian border—to the far-flung southeastern Minnesota town of Fountain—near the Iowa and Wisconsin border. I chugged my way through four-taproom-crawl marathons in Minneapolis and weathered severe thunderstorms in a two-person tent in a red dirt campground near Cuyuna Brewing in central Minnesota. After endless weekends of road trips, sing-alongs, and craft beer drinking, I took a hiatus so my spare time could stop, if only briefly, revolving around beer. During that yearlong break, twenty-five new taprooms opened, requiring me to pick the blog back up and start road tripping once again.

An editor at *The Growler*—a local beer, food, and culture publication—noticed my blog early on and asked me to start writing small features for their online content. This eventually led to more writing work and the opportunity to get to know industry folks even better.

On my twenty-third birthday, I got hired as a brand ambassador at a Minneapolis brewery that soon became my local favorite: Inbound BrewCo. A year and some change later, they hired me as their full-time marketing manager. The opportunity to work in the beer industry has humbled me, taught me more than I knew there was to know about both brewing and taprooms, and introduced me to the phenomenal people who are the backbone of Minnesota's craft beer culture.

I grew into drinking beer at a time when craft beer was plentiful. Although craft beer interest had been growing in Minneapolis for several years, by the time I turned twenty-one there were many more options to be had than just the Summit EPA and Bell's Two Hearted Ale of the generations that went before me. While those classic staples will always be a go-to craft beer on any menu and in my heart, it was the seemingly endless potential of hundreds of beers and dozens of taprooms that really attracted me to the industry. As new commercial brewers and entrepreneurs opened taprooms, I could learn alongside them. The beer was great, but the culture and possibilities enraptured me. Those possibilities are thanks to the passage of the taproom bill in 2011, which permitted breweries to pour pints of their own beers on-site. It created a craft beer boom and made brewery culture available to any patron who walked through a taproom door (or 160-plus doors in my case), and for that I will always be grateful.

In the years since I finished that first pint of Odell at a pub in Northfield, the craft beer twinkle never left my eye. The opportunity to ask questions, learn, and experiment within craft beer—whether as a casual consumer or a member of a brewery's staff—is always present. With every day at work and every taproom visit I make, I learn something new about water chemistry, fermentation science, or engineering. I also learn about human nature, stories, and joy. As a consumer-turned-brewery-office-professional, there is plenty I have yet to learn about beer and the people who drink it. This book is an articulation of what I have learned so far and the wisdom shared by the people I have met—and an invitation for you to come along on this journey with me.

Hooksetter IPA 6.6% 59 IBU
Uncommon Blonde
SPECKLED LOON
DREAMWALKER
UNCOMMON LOON
UNCOMMON LOON

INTRODUCTION

The foundations of the craft beer industry as we know it today were laid a decade ago, as interest grew in buying products that supported our local economies and whose makers we could see in the store or around the neighborhood. Craft became an economy, and beer was no exception. Craft beer was special, though, in that the taproom culture brought people together in a space where they could share their passion with fellow craft beer enthusiasts and even engage in the creative process with the brewer. With the advent of taprooms, not only could you purchase a locally made product that was full of flavor, you could drink it next to the tanks where it had been fermenting only days earlier, and do so while building camaraderie and community.

Before the emergence of a locavore economy, craft beer enthusiasts could pursue their interests and tastes only through a small number of national brands or imports. As folks came up empty-handed in their search for distinctive beer styles at their local liquor stores and watering holes, they simply made for themselves what nobody else would. Thus, the homebrewing hobby emerged. Homebrewing by amateur craftspeople gave Americans the opportunity to experience brews more flavorful than the standard domestic lagers. Many of these entrepreneurs and innovators would make the leap to brewing for commercial production and sale, and a series of changes in the state's liquor laws helped to break open the door for a revolution in Minnesota craft brewing. The proliferation of growlers, crowlers, and taprooms—all illegal in the state less than two decades ago—brought new styles and flavors to a wider audience and greatly expanded Minnesotans' beer-drinking palates.

In 2020, nearly two hundred craft breweries are operating in the state of Minnesota. The desire to gather in our own low-key social

Uncommon Loon Brewing Company in Chisago City is a popular taproom destination north of the Twin Cities.

environments and experience these exciting brews expanded from the early homebrew geeks and beer nerds to new casual drinkers looking for something fresh to try and someplace local to support. It grew from the Twin Cities to the farthest corners of outstate Minnesota. It is expanding from mostly white guys to a more diverse audience, though that project is still largely in progress. Nowadays, craft beer lovers not only frequent their own neighborhood taprooms but also travel to destination breweries because of Instagram fame and Untappd recommendations or simply to sample what a different city or neighborhood has to offer. Taprooms are the sites of wedding rehearsal dinners, reunions, surprise parties, first dates, and regular happy hours. People have adopted taprooms as their go-to social venues, and the taprooms have welcomed them in return.

The small, independent breweries that operate these taprooms pour styles ranging from light-and-easy pilsners and kölsches to triple-dry-hopped, haze-bomb IPAs; they run barrel programs to age imperial stouts and ferment funky sours; and, most importantly, they brew what their patrons want. No brewery can survive if it does not fill a niche in the market with its style, location, experience, and/or branding, and it definitely will not succeed if it cannot sell enough volume to pay the rent. All this leaves you, the taproom patron, responsible for making or breaking a brewery's success. The beers you order will determine the menu, the times you visit will determine the hours, and the pints you drink will determine whether the business lives or dies. The craft beer industry is tied to its patrons in such a way that you can see the effects of your consumer preferences on the brewery.

IN 2019, 644,655 BARRELS OF CRAFT BEER WERE BREWED IN MINNESOTA, AND 25.9 MILLION BARRELS WERE BREWED NATIONWIDE.

Over the last ten years, craft beer has disrupted the alcohol industry establishment and stolen a place in our hearts, and now it is cementing its place in Minnesota's future. Today, lobbyists seek change to support the growth of these small businesses, liquor stores reserve shelf space for new local releases, and professionals seek specialized degrees to build a career in the industry. While production and sales of craft beer still pale in comparison to that of national domestic lagers, craft brewers are staking their territory, and they don't plan to leave anytime soon.

We are fortunate to be witnessing the birth and boom of an industry—witnessing exponential growth from a tiny, five-gallon homebrew-on-your-stovetop inception. Every one of the 644,655 barrels of craft beer brewed in Minnesota in 2019 is a story of an entrepreneur and a craftsperson. While that number may seem big, my goal is to make it feel small. And, in the scope of business, it really is small. When you purchase a pint or four-pack of locally made beer, you are not contributing to some CEO's yacht fund or lining a shareholder's pocket; you are investing in a tiny slice of your neighbor's dream. From the outside, it may seem like craft beer simply arrived in your neighborhood one day, and you may be tempted to take the ubiquity of Minnesota's taprooms for granted. I hope these pages help you to see and appreciate how this industry was built by passion and perseverance so that we all might enjoy a pint together for many years to come.

CRAFT BEER DEMOGRAPHICS

According to a study conducted by the Brewers Association, a nationwide organization of American breweries, the typical craft beer enthusiast at the beginning of the twenty-first century was a thirty-nine-year-old, rich, white man. Over the succeeding two decades, the craft beer scene has been populated more and more by young people and women, as well as a more geographically and socioeconomically diverse clientele. By 2018, according to the Brewers Association's Bart Watson, the craft industry was "onboarding men and women into the category [of craft drinkers] at roughly their percentages in the population. It's not quite 50/50, and it will take decades of the same pattern to get closer to parity, but it's a start." A study of craft beer drinkers conducted between June 2016 and November 2017 found that nearly 36 percent of craft beer drinkers in Minneapolis and St. Paul were women, which was slightly above the national average of 31 percent.

Why the shift? For one, the proliferation of taprooms in a range of different neighborhoods provided new avenues of entrance into the proverbial "old boys' club" of craft beer's homebrewing roots. A person no longer had to know a homebrewer to experience craft beer. Furthermore, brewing involves STEM skills—mechanics, plumbing, and chemistry—which women weren't widely encouraged to acquire prior to 2000. The hobby also requires leisure time and disposable income, limiting it to higher socioeconomic groups. Taprooms, operating as public spaces offering a variety of beer styles, opened the access point

Taprooms are an easy place to pass an afternoon over flavorful beers. The craft beer scene has begun to diversify beyond the straight white men who dominated the early years of the industry, but it still has a long way to go.

for potential new craft beer drinkers. That's not to say craft beer has achieved total gender and socioeconomic inclusivity or equity, of course, but at least it's on the way.

Watson also commented on the racial and ethnic gaps in craft beer drinkers, noting: "Changes in craft's demographics by race/ethnicity are less positive in recent years." As much as taprooms might have literal and metaphorical open doors to any and all customers, that simply isn't enough. Breweries lack diversity in every position—from the brewers and packaging teams to the bartenders pouring your beer. Thankfully, local individuals, groups, and organizations are working to shift the numbers in Minnesota by fostering diversity, equity, and inclusion for BIPOC people in the brewing industry. Today, the Twin Cities are home to a precious few breweries owned by non-white people. Sergio Manancero, a first-generation Uruguayan American, owns La Doña Cervecería in Minneapolis; St. Paul's Vine Park Brewing is the self-described "only Hmong-owned brewery in the world"; and Ramsey Louder (previously of New Holland and Dangerous Man) opened ONE Fermentary & Taproom in 2019, becoming the first Black man to have ownership in a brewery in Minneapolis.

In the wake of George Floyd's murder in May 2020, however, the systemic racism upon which our country is built was revealed in Minnesota's brewing industry. Notably, Ramsey Louder and several of his colleagues left their positions at ONE Fermentary. Each employee made a public statement about their departure, citing differences of opinion with other ownership regarding how to best realize the mission of ONE to be a truly inclusive space. The brewpub of their dreams did not live up to the standards they had once set for it. ONE has since closed its doors indefinitely.

This small number of businesses and organizations signals what I hope is a shift in our brewing community and a sign of a more just and equitable industry to come. But, as we learned in the case of ONE Fermentary, hiring and tokenizing a few BIPOC employees is not nearly the end of the road; the craft beer industry still has plenty of work to do.

A BRIEF HISTORY OF BEER AND CRAFT BREWING

THE NATIONAL STORY

Centuries ago, people brewed beer not for its magical capacity to build community or to explore flavor. Women, servants, and enslaved people were assigned the chore of brewing low-proof ale because it was safer to drink than water. German immigrants in the mid-nineteenth century brought more modern brewing traditions to America's shores, and big beer began to boom.

Then, in 1919, we encountered a watershed moment in a long history of alcohol regulation in this country: the Eighteenth Amendment to the US Constitution. This amendment prohibited the production, importation, transportation, and sale of alcoholic beverages throughout the United States and its territories. It went into effect in January 1920 and lasted through 1933, at which time the Twenty-First Amendment repealed it.

Prohibition killed most small breweries that had been operating prior to 1920, while the big ones got through by brewing soda and "near beer" (and perhaps a bit of under-the-table beer brewing, too). The Eighteenth Amendment also inspired a league of law-bending homebrewers.

Austin Lunn, head brewer for HammerHeart Brewing in Lino Lakes, is a bit of a history buff, and he observes that prior to Prohibition, American breweries mirrored European beer culture, where "each community had its own brewery, and that's where everyone went to get their beer." After Prohibition, the few big breweries that survived the dry spell monopolized the market. Indeed, the decades following the repeal of Prohibition saw efficiency and uniformity become the modus operandi of large commercial brewers working to stay afloat. A small number of large regional or national breweries dominated the market, and by 1978, the nation was home to the lowest number of breweries since Prohibition. However, this uniformity and a dearth of great locally produced beer helped spur a new generation of homebrewers to pick up the mantle.

Writing for the National Museum of American History's blog in 2018, historian Theresa McCulla described the changes in the beer industry during the second half of the twentieth century:

Prohibition led to tragic scenes such as this one, in New York City, as agents pour beer into the sewers following a raid, circa 1921. *Library of Congress Prints and Photographs Division*

"Paradoxically, the bland homogeneity of mid-century American beer was the perfect motivation for things to get much more interesting. A handful of enthusiasts discovered the venerable beer cultures of Europe during military or educational travels abroad. They returned to the United States with brewing manuals and embarked on an under-the-radar hobby (homebrewing remained illegal until 1979), adapting hardware store equipment and repurposing supermarket ingredients to make better beer."

When homebrewing was finally legalized under federal law in 1979, people began taking matters of available beer styles into their own hands. Homebrewers relied on a handful of guidebooks to learn the craft, but Charlie Papazian's 1984 book, *The Complete Joy of Home Brewing*, became—and remains—an essential homebrewing text. Papazian also founded the Association of Brewing (now the Brewers Association), the American Homebrewers Association, several beer and brewing publications, the Great American Beer Festival, and the World Beer Cup, further building a community and culture around American craft beer. Papazian's work inspired a wave of homebrewers who would become the godparents of the modern craft beer movement. McCulla writes that, according to Papazian, "90% of craft breweries were founded by brewers who began as homebrewers." If you ever meet him, please buy Charlie a beer.

Building on the efforts of homebrewing entrepreneurs and some adventurous breweries, the growth of craft beer in the United States has been swift and far reaching. Craft beer production more than doubled nationwide between 2011 and 2019. While the big national breweries continue to dominate the market with their American lagers, today craft represents about 14 percent of the overall market share for beer, and the craft segment grew by 4 percent from 2018 to 2019 while overall beer sales were down—further illustrating the resilience of craft beer.

THE MINNESOTA STORY

In 2010, Minnesota had nine breweries in operation—Schell's, Summit, Lake Superior, Finnegans, Surly, Brau Brothers, Flat Earth, Lift Bridge,

Originally known as Cave Brewery, the Schmidt Brewing Company began serving up beers in St. Paul before Minnesota was a state. It is shown here in about 1905, five years after the brewery was purchased by Jacob Schmidt. *Photo from Minnesota Historical Society Collections*

and Fulton—plus about the same number of brewpubs producing their own beer. Going back 150 years, to the first decades of statehood, the growth of breweries and beer drinking in Minnesota had been led largely by its German immigrant communities. A strong temperance movement within the state, however, coincided with a gradual decline in the number of breweries in the early twentieth century, before Prohibition all but wiped out the brewing scene in Minnesota, as elsewhere. (The Volstead Act, the law that enacted the Eighteenth Amendment, was named for Andrew Volstead, a US representative from Minnesota's seventh district, who authored the bill.) It took decades for the state's beer industry to recover, and for nearly a century, Minnesotans relied on a small number of breweries, such as Minneapolis Brewing Company and the Schmidt Brewery, for local product.

It wasn't until 2011, and the passage of the taproom bill by the Minnesota state legislature, that we saw a surge in the number of breweries in our state. The law allowed breweries not just to brew and sell their beer for off-sale, but also to operate a taproom immediately

TIMELINE OF KEY EVENTS IN MODERN MINNESOTA CRAFT BREWING HISTORY

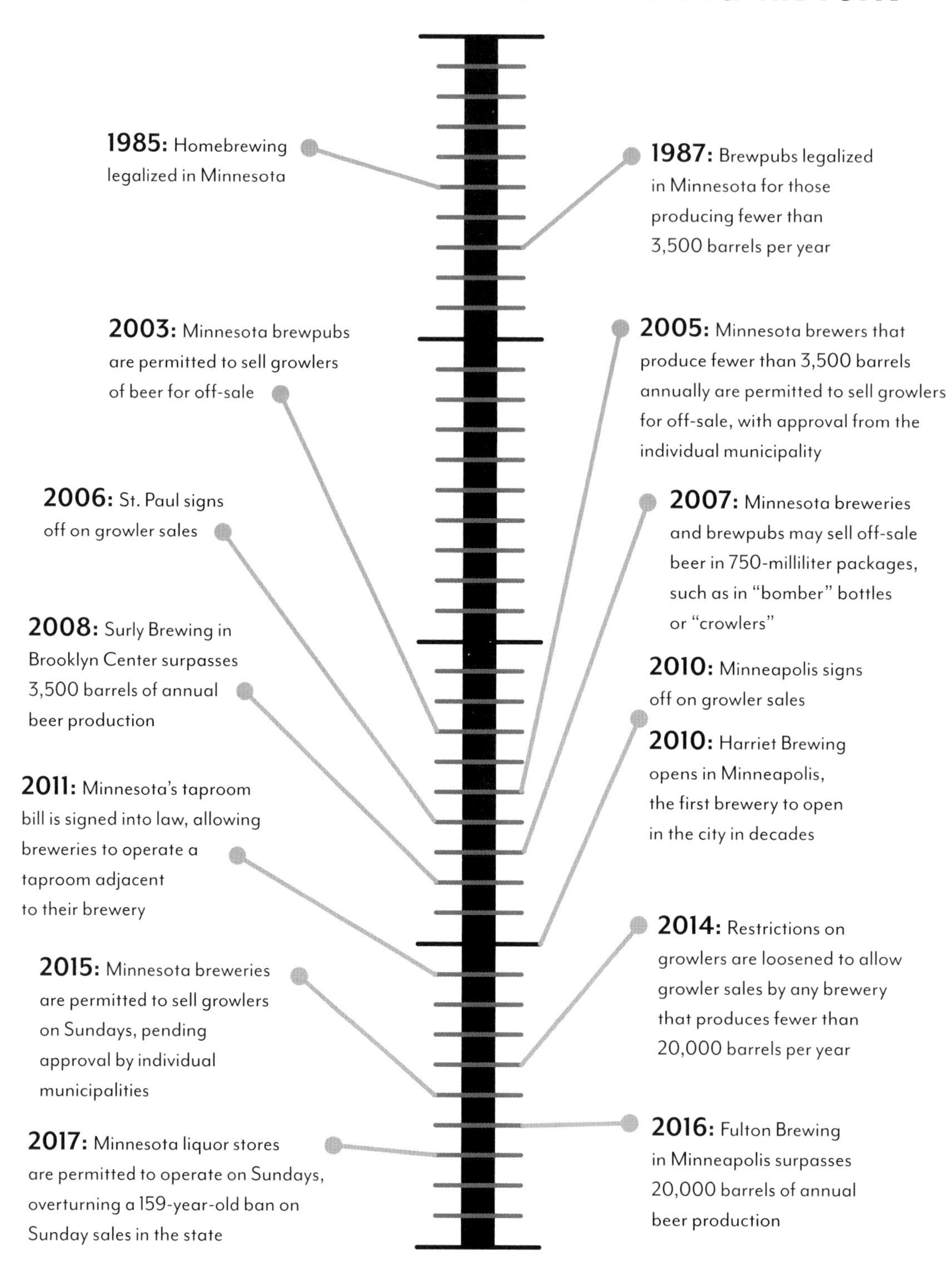

adjacent to the brewery. This meant that, finally, a brewer could pour beer for their consumers at their very own bar. It would completely transform Minnesota's craft beer industry.

An overview of recent Minnesota brewing history illustrates the slow progress Minnesota brewers made in recovering from the "Prohibition hangover," as Laura Mullen of Bent Paddle Brewing in Duluth calls it.

The first step toward modernizing Minnesota's restrictive liquor laws came in 1985 with the legalization of homebrewing—six years after it was permitted by federal law. (This slow move to action portends Minnesota's plodding path to loosening restrictions around craft breweries decades later. At least we beat Alabama and Mississippi to the homebrewing punch, as those states waited until 2013 to legalize the hobby.) Two years later, in 1987, the state legislature passed a law that allowed brewpubs to legally operate in Minnesota. While these businesses were permitted to brew and sell their own beer on-site, they were limited to a maximum production of 3,500 barrels per year. Brewpubs, unlike our modern taprooms, can also sell wine, liquor, and beer produced by other manufacturers.

Several brewpubs opened in Minnesota in the wake of the 1987 brewpub bill, including Rock Bottom, Town Hall, Great Waters, Herkimer, Barley John's, Fitger's in Duluth, Backwater Brewing in Winona, and others. These brewpubs produced and sold their own beer while also selling liquor and food. As Doug Hoverson wrote in his book *Land of Amber Waters*, brewpubs are restaurants first and foremost, but their impact on our beer industry is significant. Even so, while brewpubs both fostered and satiated Minnesotans' taste for craft beer, the opportunity for true craft beer geekery was limited. The brewpubs focused on food as their main moneymaker, and restaurant-style seating and service are not as conducive to learning about the beer as compared to the taproom environment we have come to know and love. Another key step toward broadening Minnesotans' access to craft beer came in 2003, when the state permitted brewpubs to sell growlers, or 64-ounce jugs of beer, for off-sale.

Town Hall Brewery, in the Seven Corners District of Minneapolis, was an early and influential presence among Twin Cities brewpubs.

While brewpubs were establishing a market for on-site craft beer drinking, production breweries were also building momentum toward further expanding the local offerings. Revenue for these breweries came from bottle sales in liquor stores and kegs tapped at restaurants. The big shift arrived in 2005, when any brewer that produced fewer than 3,500 barrels of beer annually gained permission to sell growlers for off-sale. This provided new opportunities for breweries that did not sell enough volume to justify investing in an automated bottling or canning line. However, each municipality had to approve growler sales by breweries within their jurisdictions. That approval came quickly for St. Paul brewers, in 2006. Minneapolis didn't follow suit until 2010, but the city's approval of growler sales ultimately helped spur the opening of Harriet Brewing on Minnehaha Avenue, the first brewery to open in the city in decades. Although Harriet Brewing closed in November 2016, its impact is still felt throughout the local beer world through the personnel the brewery brought into the industry and who went on to work at and open new breweries in Minnesota.

Beginning in 2007, Minnesota breweries and brewpubs were permitted to sell off-sale beer in 750-milliliter (about 25-ounce) packages, paving the way for "bomber" bottles. In 2012, Colorado's Oskar Blues Brewery introduced "crowlers" (a portmanteau from *can* and *growler*) to the beer market, allowing breweries to more easily and inexpensively package beer in smaller volumes than growlers. The crowlers we use in Minnesota still fit the 750-milliliter requirement that allowed bomber bottles, whereas breweries in most other states use 32-ounce crowlers.

The production limitations of the original growler bill were hit just a few years after it passed into law. In December 2008, after being in business for less than three years, Surly Brewing exceeded 3,500 barrels of annual production, thus putting it beyond the realm of legal growler sales at the time. This impressive milestone by the innovative brewery also marked the beginning of the end for Minnesota's tight restrictions on craft breweries and helped clear the way for a craft beer revolution in the state.

The "growler cap" for breweries was eventually increased from 3,500 barrels per year to 20,000 barrels in 2014 (a brewery can sell only 750 barrels in growlers per year, regardless of its production volume), but it still wasn't enough for some breweries. In 2016, Fulton Brewing of Minneapolis became the first of the new wave of craft breweries to surpass the 20,000-barrel production limit, thus disallowing them from selling growlers. They celebrated with a "Death of the Growler" party featuring live music and commemorative T-shirts.

Prior to the passage of the growler and 750-milliliter bottle bills, Minnesota brewers either could produce beer to sell at bars and liquor stores or they could function as a brewpub, in which case they would forgo the ability to distribute altogether. The new laws brought minor advancements by introducing another revenue stream for smaller brewers, but they weren't much good for larger breweries. Any brewer with a dream of selling beer widely to the masses had to invest in packaging equipment, delivery vans, off-site marketing collateral, and much more. One alternative to all this self-investment was to sign a contract with a beer distributor, which cut into a brewery's already slim profits. Compared to the ability of today's brewers to sell pints of beer mere yards from their brewhouses, the situation for any prospective brewer prior to the growler bill of 2003 and, especially, the 2011 taproom bill was challenging.

The Taproom Bill

After years of lobbying and hard work on the part of Minnesota brewery owners and their dedicated patrons, the Minnesota state legislature signed bill H.F. No. 1326—the "taproom bill"—into law in May 2011. The law allowed Minnesota breweries to operate a taproom adjacent to their brewery where they could sell beer for consumption on-site. Simply put, the law thoroughly transformed the landscape for Minnesota craft beer. Its passage was a hard-won battle against a system and mindset that were stuck in the temperance and prohibition movements of previous centuries.

The new law vastly expanded the available playing field for Minnesota brewers and craft beer lovers. Not only did it allow existing brewers to sell their products to be enjoyed on-site where they could interact with customers and build a community of beer enthusiasts, it opened up a substantial new revenue stream. Furthermore, the bill incentivized others to open new breweries by offering a built-in source of income where the profit margin was far greater than in distribution and off-sale growler models. The taproom bill was a necessary leap forward for any Minnesota brewer who hoped to compete with other

American craft breweries, like Odell or Tallgrass, that were becoming increasingly popular on our home turf.

The bill came about in large part thanks to the efforts of Surly Brewing and its owner, Omar Ansari; the taproom bill is commonly referred to as the "Surly Bill" for that reason. Ansari's reasons for pushing the bill forward weren't entirely unselfish. The brewery that we now know and love for its immense destination taproom in Minneapolis and its flagship Furious IPA (among other noteworthy offerings) originally operated out of an industrial abrasives factory owned by Ansari's parents in suburban Brooklyn Center. Within just a few years of opening in February 2006, the brewery owners knew they wouldn't be able to keep up with demand in their current location.

Ansari had a vision for a brewery that not only could handle Surly's growing production needs but also would be a destination for lovers of craft beer. This vision was the impetus behind his efforts to change the laws, and his advocacy and persistent lobbying on behalf of the brewing community helped ensure its passage. When Surly opened its multimillion-dollar taproom in December 2014, it created a space unlike anything Minnesota beer drinkers had seen before. In addition to building a massive, visually stunning facility with tremendous food options, Surly was able to enjoy unprecedented growth in beer production. In one year, it went from producing 38,906 barrels to 62,432 barrels—an increase of 160 percent.

Most importantly, though, Surly's vision for a special beer-drinking experience opened the door for so many more brewers to follow their dreams. Between the passage of the taproom bill in May 2011 and the opening of Surly's destination brewery in December 2014, no fewer than forty taprooms opened across the state of Minnesota. That number more than tripled in the subsequent five years. As Minneapolis mayor R. T. Rybak put it, "It's tough to find any law changes that have had such a tangible, visible impact on just people in the community as the Surly bill, which rightly is good for those of us who like really good beer. But it's really been a jobs bill."

The first brewery to take advantage of the new law was Leech Lake Brewing, which had opened in Walker in 2010 and added a

Proudly Minneapolis made, Fulton Brewing has long been a fixture of the city's taproom boom. The brewery opened its taproom in the North Loop neighborhood in 2012 and has been growing ever since.

small tasting room after the bill passed. (The brewery closed in 2015.) Lift Bridge in Stillwater was the second brewery to follow suit, opening a taproom in October 2011 after operating as an off-sale-only brewery since 2008. Opening a taproom was just the beginning of Lift Bridge's growth. In 2010, it brewed 2,000 barrels. In 2018, seven years after the taproom opened, it brewed 14,425 barrels on-site and another 5,000 via contracts with other breweries—an absolute testament to the craft beer boom. Similar stories can be told of other breweries that existed prior to the taproom bill. They had built their businesses on passion and survived on bottle, keg, and growler sales before opening a taproom was even an option. With the passage of the taproom bill, their capacity to sell beer at greater margins increased, and the intimate tasting space enhanced consumer interest in their beers and businesses.

"IT'S HARD TO OVERSTATE THE IMPACT OF THE 'SURLY BILL' ON THE CRAFT BEER INDUSTRY IN MINNESOTA. BESIDES LEGISLATIVE LEGITIMACY, THE BILL WAS DESIGNED TO GIVE NEW SMALL BUSINESSES A CASH FLOW, ALLOWING THEM TO CREATE A WORTHWHILE HEADQUARTERS TO INTERACT WITH CONSUMERS, WHILE FOSTERING COMMUNITY AROUND THEIR BRAND."

—JOHN GARLAND, *THE GROWLER*, APRIL 2013

In addition to existing breweries that were able to make the transition from a distribution model to include a taproom component, other breweries that were in development at the time were able to pivot toward this more diverse business model. Both Bent Paddle in Duluth and Indeed in Minneapolis had been planning to open as production breweries prior to the taproom bill, and they were able to adjust their plans and incorporate taprooms into their facilities. Even breweries that had found a model of success through distribution embraced the taproom concept as a way to expand both their business and their connections to the beer-drinking community.

In the years following the taproom bill, Minnesota's craft beer industry grew exponentially, with many new players entering the arena, and we found our place among the nation's top brewing locations. According to the Brewers Association, the number of craft breweries in Minnesota increased from 35 in 2011 to 196 in 2019—giving the state 4.7 craft breweries per capita of adults aged twenty-one and older, the fourteenth highest in the nation. Minnesota also ranked twelfth in the nation for total barrels of craft beer produced in 2019. The craft boom here has been even more dramatic than that in our famously beer-loving neighbor, Wisconsin. Though Wisconsin produces more total craft beer (883,648 barrels to Minnesota's 644,655), Minnesota craft beer production increased by a whopping 279 percent between 2011 and 2019, whereas Wisconsin's growth was

A patron enjoying an array of tasty brews at the Lift Bridge Brewing Company taproom in Stillwater. Lift Bridge began as a production brewery in 2008 and added a taproom in 2011 shortly after passage of the taproom bill.

less than half that over the same period (128 percent). Of course, Wisconsin's craft beer production was much larger than Minnesota's in 2011, but our home state has seen a rapid increase over a short period of time. In 2011, Wisconsin had more than twice as many craft breweries as Minnesota (73 vs. 35), whereas today, the gap is negligible (205 to 196, as of 2019). For years skeptics have predicted that the bubble will burst, but new breweries continue to open across our state, and only a dozen or so have closed during this period.

With the growth in the number of breweries and taprooms during the 2010s, consumers were able to embrace craft beer as a hobby and a culture without having to become chemistry-minded homebrewers and investing in all the necessary equipment and ingredients. They could participate in pub crawls, beer trades, meetups with friends, and more. For some, taprooms were the entry point to a fascination with craft beer. Not only did they provide a social gathering space and general exposure to craft beer, they also allowed for low-stakes sampling. A taproom patron does not have to invest in the cost of a six-pack to try out a new-to-them style—they can just ask for a sample from the bartender before committing to a full pint.

Tom Whisenand, cofounder of Indeed Brewing, commented in 2013, "When we first opened the doors [to our taproom], people came in and they had their first Indeed beer here. Then they went out to their local liquor stores and local bars and restaurants and said, 'Hey, do you have Indeed? Can you get Indeed?'" As such, breweries were able to use the taproom environment as a launching pad for expanding their distribution market as well.

The taproom bill helped to foster a whole culture of craft beer in Minnesota. Even those not engaged in the culture are often touched by it in some way: through a friend's beer fridge, a charity event hosted in a taproom, or a happy hour planned by a coworker.

THE LEGAL INTRICACIES

Although the taproom bill spurred exponential growth in Minnesota's craft beer scene, it would be a mistake to assume that the new law instantaneously created a landscape in which independent craft brewers could pursue their dreams with abandon. We're talking about liquor in Minnesota, so there were more than a few catches.

The new law permitted Minnesota municipalities to issue licenses for brewers' taprooms, which "authorize[d] on-sale of malt liquor produced by the brewer for consumption on the premises of or adjacent to one brewery location owned by the brewer." But the law was followed up by a handful of limitations: brewers can have only one taproom in Minnesota, meaning there is no opportunity to expand to a second location within the state; brewers may not exceed 250,000 barrels per year, a limit that's not *yet* a threat to Minnesota's breweries (Summit

Brewing in St. Paul produced the most barrels in the state in 2019, with 128,000 barrels); and brewers may not sell any alcoholic beverages that were not brewed on-site.

In addition, in the same year the Minnesota state legislature passed the taproom bill, members declined to pass another law that would have allowed brewpubs to sell kegs of their beer to other bars and restaurants. And as recently as the 2019 legislative session, several key laws failed to make the omnibus liquor bill, including a proposal to raise the growler cap and to allow breweries to sell off-sale beer in packages smaller than 750 milliliters.

Why so many caveats and regulations for an industry that was clearly booming elsewhere in the country? In part, it's because the legislation in Minnesota has been pieced together slowly over time. According to Evan Sallee of Fair State Brewing Cooperative—who also has a law degree and is the current president of the Minnesota Craft Brewers Guild—the craft beer landscape has changed quickly and dramatically in a relatively short period of time, and the laws haven't kept pace with consumer expectations. "There have been discrete things breweries have asked for, and every party has asked for small tweaks here and there," he says. "And as a result, we have a code that has been built up without thinking holistically. So, you have exceptions on exceptions that don't necessarily make a lot of sense in totality but just have inertia behind them." Sallee further points out that, with so many interested parties and so many businesses that have been built on the status quo, "It's extremely hard to change even if it might make sense as a whole. ... Even if it's great for consumers in the long run to make certain changes, that has real impacts on people's livelihoods and their ability to operate a business day to day."

Industry groups such as the Minnesota Licensed Beverage Association and the Minnesota Beer Wholesalers Association have lobbied hard to limit the growth of craft brewers in order to protect their own business interests. These associations represent manufacturers, wholesalers, and suppliers, whose business models and revenues are built around a three-tier system. This system was put in place in the pre-Prohibition era as a way to protect distributors from "big bad" corporate breweries. Today, however, most Minnesota breweries are small businesses started by enthusiastic hobbyists-turned-professionals, while distributors are often run with funding from large, corporate breweries. The tables have turned, and it is now the breweries that need protection from the "big bad" distributors in order to survive.

The practice of Minnesota legislators stifling brewers goes back to the repeal of Prohibition. When the Twenty-First Amendment overturned Prohibition in 1933, each state gained the right to regulate alcohol however it saw fit. As a result, regulations vary widely from state to state—the cost of licenses, off-sale packaging permitted at the brewery, what other alcoholic beverages may be sold, the list goes on. But, as Jeff O'Brien—dubbed "Minnesota's brewery lawyer" and the go-to expert for deciphering, fighting, and changing Minnesota brewery laws—explained in his 2017 article in the *Mitchell Hamline Law Review*, there's one thing that most states have in common: the three-tier system (cue dramatic music).

Systems are usually boring, but this one is filled with drama, politics, and intrigue. The three-tier system—which encompasses the brewer, the beer distributor, and the retailer—is enforced by a set of laws and regulations that aims to prevent monopolies. The three-tier system may help to accomplish this goal, but it also tears down small businesses in the process.

In the early days of Minnesota's post-Prohibition beer industry, brewers were often trapped into binding, everlasting contracts with beer distributors. Not much has changed since then. Nowadays, an exchange of emails or a sharing of beer samples could land a brewer in a binding agreement that is practically impossible to escape. At least now, with nearly a century of learning opportunities under their belts, brewers know how to better protect themselves from dubious relationships, but they are still on the losing end of most distribution contracts. O'Brien calls it out: "When it comes to local craft breweries, [distribution contracts] get used as a weapon against

William Figge, general superintendent and brewmaster of the Theodore Hamm Brewing Company, drawing the first stein of legalized beer in St. Paul following the repeal of Prohibition in 1933. *Photo from Minnesota Historical Society Collections*

them." Steve Hindy, president and cofounder of Brooklyn Brewery, seconded the potential drawbacks of working with a beer distributor in a 2014 *New York Times* op-ed piece. "The contracts not only prevent other companies from distributing a company's beers," he explained, "but also give the distributor virtual carte blanche to decide how the beer is sold and placed in stores and bars—in essence, the distributor owns the brand inside that state." A distributor relationship is not by definition bad for the brewer, and it can be a fruitful business partnership. Unfortunately, the protections that are built into the contracts effectively only shield the larger and more powerful distributor. Small breweries are left vulnerable.

The distributor-brewery relationship is codified into state law via the Minnesota Beer Brewers and Wholesalers Act (Minnesota Statutes chapter 325B). Within the act, brewers are skewered with language that greatly limits their ability to get out of a distribution contract. O'Brien writes, "without a showing of 'good cause' [for breaking the contract], the Act requires a brewer to pay its wholesaler 'reasonable compensation for the value of the wholesaler's business with relationship to the terminated brand or brands.' Given that the Act fails to define 'reasonable compensation,' the brewer is thus left with the choice of paying the wholesaler's ransom to release its brands or to engage in a costly arbitration proceeding to ultimately ascertain the amount to be paid."

In a 2015 blog post, O'Brien further emphasized how Minnesota law fosters an unhealthy relationship between brewers and distributors, writing that the state "artificially limits the growth of new breweries and results in concentrations of brands in certain areas (such as Minneapolis and St. Paul) instead of spreading distribution across the state as a whole." As Hindy succinctly put it in his 2014 *New York Times* op-ed piece: "The success or failure of a beer should depend on whether consumers like it—not on whether archaic distribution laws prevent them from finding it in the first place."

The state's liquor laws further hinder the growth of craft breweries by limiting consumer choices, such as by not allowing consumers to purchase four- or six-packs directly from a taproom or neighborhood brewery. The purpose of this prohibition is to protect liquor stores against beer producers becoming direct competitors and undercutting prices. While Fair State's Evan Sallee respects the history of such laws as a way of protecting smaller mom-and-pop liquor stores, these same laws now create problems for smaller breweries that are trying to grow their businesses to meet consumer demand. Sallee explains: "Liquor stores want to be able to get a product from their local brewery, but that brewery can't justify the investment in a canning line because there aren't enough local liquor stores to support that investment. So, being able to sell it directly to the consumer, I think, would go a long way to allowing these smaller brewers to compete."

O'Brien says that one solution is the small brewer exemption. It doesn't exist in Minnesota yet, but in other states, exemptions let brewers out of distribution contracts while preventing the distributor from holding the business for ransom. He writes, "Small-brewer exemptions serve the purpose of relieving small craft brewers from some of the more onerous franchise-termination provisions of beer-distribution laws while preserving the protections afforded to distributors who are susceptible to strong-arm tactics from large 'macro' breweries."

Still, most alcohol-related legislative reform in Minnesota is halted by the power of a coalition of wholesalers, retailers, and teamsters—"everybody, basically, except for the breweries and the distilleries," says O'Brien. The three-tier system was a long time in the making, and—if the folks in power have their way—it will be around for generations to come. O'Brien adds, "nobody will push any liquor bill over there [at the capitol] unless the coalition agrees." The brewery tier is just not as politically sophisticated or as financially strong as the distribution and retail tiers.

Ultimately, O'Brien believes that changing the system requires "a top-to-bottom review of all the liquor laws in the state." Otherwise, he continues, Minnesota's restrictive laws will send businesses across state lines. "If we are going to only allow one taproom per brewery," he says, "they're going to start opening up locations in other states, and those jobs and that tax revenue are going there." Thus, Indeed Brewing's decision to open a Milwaukee location and Lupulin expanding to South Dakota could be the harbingers of a larger trend.

To some degree, the recent track record of breweries' legislative successes is promising. O'Brien says, "The boom in the market here is largely attributable to the repeal of some very antiquated, restrictive laws that disfavored the manufacturing tier." Recent pro-brewer legislation that has exempted small breweries from the three-tier system includes self-distribution rights within a certain barrelage production; growler and 750-milliliter off-premise sales; and the allowance of taprooms.

Why the shift? Maybe brewers are changing the hearts and minds of our politicians with their sinful but delicious concoctions. More likely, argues O'Brien, the paradigm shift stems from the same source as so many other cultural changes: time. "It's more of a generational thing than a partisan thing," he says. As younger generations enter the political sphere, legislative votes may swing further in favor of breweries. Many communities have adopted breweries into their lives over the past decade and have seen the cultural value of craft beer firsthand. Exposure to the positive effects of craft beer and taprooms is gradually softening hearts and dispelling fears about the beer business.

Recent history also shows that the dedication of a few individuals can go a long way. O'Brien remembers a time when Mayor R. T. Rybak and city council member Gary Schiff wanted to put Minneapolis on the map by cultivating our own midwestern version of Portland, Oregon. O'Brien says, "a key piece of that [vision] was the brewery scene."

Putting his legislation where his mouth was, Schiff sponsored the "Brew Beer Here" ordinance that allowed the sale of growlers on Minneapolis brewery premises. Passed in August 2010, the ordinance facilitated brewery operation within Minneapolis city limits and led to the opening of Harriet Brewing.

Furthermore, in 2011, Schiff introduced an amendment to a local ordinance that overturned a Prohibition-era regulation forbidding breweries in Minneapolis from operating within three hundred feet of houses of worship. As a result, Dangerous Man Brewing was able to open a brewery on the corner of Thirteenth Avenue and Second Street in Northeast Minneapolis in 2013. O'Brien laughs as he recollects: "I can remember being at that city council hearing, and the members of the church were so convinced that there were going to be prostitutes across the street on Sunday mornings and people passed out in the gutter and how the city council was godless."

In fact, since opening, Dangerous Man established a volunteer program to engage their loyal patrons with the community. Their regular volunteer partners include Free Bikes 4 Kidz, Brewing a Better Forest, and Light the Night with the Leukemia & Lymphoma Society. And it's been good for business. According to a 2017 *Mpls.St.Paul Magazine* article by Dara Moskowitz Grumdahl, "In their business plan they hoped to sell 100 pints a day; on a good Saturday nowadays they sell several thousand."

Overcoming decades of perceptions and regulations grounded in the temperance-minded mentality of a century ago, breweries have become vital parts of our communities in the twenty-first century. They serve as meeting sites, community organizers, fundraisers, and valued shared spaces. Despite the efforts of "big beer" and certain state legislators, craft breweries are paving their own way forward, and bringing some tasty beverages along for the ride.

DRINKING BEER TOGETHER

The ability of breweries to open their own taprooms is unquestionably a major root cause for Minnesota's craft beer boom. A taproom serves as a focal point for a craft brewery and allows the business to orient itself as a neighborhood establishment. In addition, taprooms provide a vital revenue stream in a fiercely competitive industry. Without the financial foundation of a bar and dedicated tap lines from which to serve their brews, few of Minnesota's current craft brewery owners would have even considered opening a place of their own. In many instances, the taproom is a brewery's main (or in some cases, sole) business.

The centrality of a taproom to a brand is one of the keys to success for a modern craft brewery, and many breweries will focus their sales and marketing efforts on drawing people to the taproom. Not only does the space provide an immersive experience in the brewery's brand—from the interior design to exclusive tap handle rights to the language on the beer menu—the taproom is also a source of great financial opportunity. Although building a taproom can be a significant investment, the beer halls will hopefully pay for themselves (and the brewing equipment that supports them) in improved margins on pints sold. Profits are not lost to distributors, bars, and markups when the beer is poured in a brewery's own taproom. As beer and legal expert Jeff O'Brien states: "the craft beer movement is changing the paradigm of how we purchase and consume alcohol. You might go to the liquor store once in a while to get something, but a lot of folks want to come to a taproom. They want to sample different beers, and they may bring a crowler or growler back home. It used to be that you were a Bud drinker or a Miller drinker or a Leinie's guy or whatever. That's not the way it is anymore."

Dangerous Man Brewing is a small, extremely popular neighborhood taproom in Northeast Minneapolis.

The branding opportunities offered by a taproom should not be underestimated. A sense of craft, locality, and experience can be evoked by a single visit to a taproom, which fosters repeat customers at both the bar and the liquor store. Brad Glynn of Lift Bridge Brewery says taprooms are a pivotal point of contact between beer makers and beer drinkers: "It's your way to tell the story of your brand in the most authentic way possible to the consumer." He waxes a bit romantic as he explains how seeing the equipment from your spot at the bar, hearing cans and kegs clank, and smelling malt are all part of the taproom experience that help connect the customer to the brewery.

In their taprooms, breweries also have control over factors such as the diversity of tap lists, the timing of pulling beers from the tap lines, and how bartenders talk about the beers with the customers. Compared to bars that offer products from a variety of different sources, bartenders at taprooms can recommend a beverage based on a patron's personal preference without sending them away from the brand.

Small-scale production is also more feasible for brewers when they have a taproom in which to sell the beer they hope to produce, providing opportunity for a more varied and experimental selection. With canning and distribution, a brewery is limited by economies of scale, and distribution relies on a consistent lineup of canned or bottled offerings in order to avoid the additional costs and time involved in introducing new releases. In contrast, taprooms present the perfect laboratory for experimentation and one-off recipes. The risks are relatively small—if small-batch experiments are less popular than projected, brewers are stuck with only a handful of kegs—and the creative possibilities are seemingly endless. Even for breweries that choose to distribute, the taproom can serve as a testing ground for new beers. In addition, taproom patrons value the early access to new releases and the opportunity to have a voice in the development of a brewery's offerings—a phenomenon that keeps the business feeling like it's craft.

KEYS TO A SUCCESSFUL TAPROOM

Taprooms are much more than a building in which to pour and drink beer. While they are great places for consumers to keep an eye on the newest beer trends, they are also a meaningful physical space designed around social gathering. They function as a type of third place in our neighborhoods—an unassuming space where people can meet up and be in community. A taproom is a place to enjoy food trucks, see leashed dogs sitting at their owners' feet, and hear local bands.

Every taproom takes a slightly different shape than the one in the next neighborhood or town over. Taprooms alter their offerings to best suit their local market. A taproom located in a city or town without a strong food truck community, for example, might partner with local restaurants for free delivery. Some will focus on hosting big beer release events, whereas others are more tuned in to the Tuesday night trivia crowd. Each design feature, special event, and new addition to the menu contributes to a mosaic of experiences that defines a taproom.

The Taproom as Third Place

The "third place" is a concept of community building and civic engagement that identifies spaces outside of home and work where people engage and interact with their communities. As Rebekah White explained in *New Zealand Geographic* in 2018, "your first place is your home, and your second is your workplace, but your third place is where you relax in public, where you encounter familiar faces and make new acquaintances. These places are cheap or free. They're open to people from all walks of life."

Taprooms are a natural third place in the lives of many Minnesotans and of Americans everywhere. They function as a gathering hub for folks from a range of social groups; the environment is easygoing and welcoming; and the taproom is a comfortable space to pass some time in convivial joy. The average American of legal drinking age lives within ten miles of a brewery, according to the Brewers Association, making the taproom a readily available space for millions of people.

Ray Oldenburg pioneered the concept of the third place in his 1989 book, *The Great Good Place*. His characteristics of the third place are:

> **On Neutral Ground:** "There must be places where individuals may come and go as they please, in which none are required to play host, and in which all feel at home and comfortable."

> **The Third Place Is a Leveler:** "A place that is a leveler is, by its nature, an inclusive place. It is accessible to the general public and does not set formal criteria of membership and exclusion."

A taproom is a cherished gathering space for a community, a key business channel for a brewery, and a perfect place to enjoy great craft beer. Forager Brewery in Rochester is just one example of the many successful taprooms that have been popping up around Minnesota in the last decade.

Conversation Is the Main Activity: "Nothing more clearly indicates a third place than that the talk there is good; that it is lively, scintillating, colorful, and engaging."

Accessibility and Accommodation: "Third places that render the best and fullest service are those to which one may go alone at almost any time of the day or evening with assurance that acquaintances will be there."

The Regulars: "Third places are dominated by their regulars but not necessarily in a numerical sense. It is the regulars, whatever their number on any given occasion, who feel at home in a place and set the tone of conviviality."

A Low Profile: "Plainness, especially on the inside of third places, also serves to discourage pretention among those who gather there. A non-pretentious décor corresponds with and encourages leveling and the abandonment of social pretense."

The Mood Is Playful: "It may be an impromptu gathering with no set activity at which everyone stays longer than intended because they are enjoying themselves and hate to leave. The urge to return, recreate, and recapture the experience is there. Invariably the suggestion is made, 'Let's do this again!' The third place exists because of that urge."

A Home Away from Home: "Using the first and second definitions of home (according to my Webster's), the third place does not qualify, being neither 1) the 'family's place of residence' or 2) that 'social unit formed by a family living together.' But the third definition of home as offering 'a congenial environment' is more apt to apply to the average third place than the average family residence."

If you've visited any of Minnesota's many neighborhood taprooms, odds are that you've noticed the presence of at least some of these features of a third place. They are communal and engaging and don't ask too much of you. These are the characteristics that made me fall in love with taprooms and craft beer in tandem.

It's no coincidence that so many Minnesotans connect over brewery experiences. Whether someone is on a quest to visit every taproom in the state or is simply communing with strangers over the brewery T-shirts they are wearing, taprooms are a form of connection to both our state and each other. I remember details about small towns I visited once for the sole purpose of going to the local taproom, and those memories serve as a point of connection and conversation with someone new.

A brewery's taproom must be congenial to be successful. The most memorable taproom experiences I've had are not necessarily connected to the beer, but are instead due to the pleasant and sociable interactions

I enjoyed there. Even among groups that are not socially connected, a taproom is filled with kindred spirits, enjoying libations and socializing in harmony.

Taproom Design

Taprooms evoke a rich experience of a brewery's style; their atmosphere enhances patrons' appreciation for the beers and the stories behind them. Taproom design is a major contributor to such experiences. Many are designed around values of coziness, connection, and craft. Reclaimed barnwood paneling, benches for seating, and warm-colored wood tables are common. Few taprooms that I know have furniture that looks like it came from the same big box store as a chain restaurant's furnishings. Regardless of how they accomplish it, taprooms strive to carve out design aesthetics that are distinct from other commercial spaces.

A taproom is like a brewery's living room, and that means it will always be built with love and intention. Some are even thoughtfully produced by professional designers. Atom Pechman, the owner/

The chalkboard at Indeed Brewing Company's Minneapolis taproom welcomes patrons to the space.

designer/fabricator at Form From Form art and design studio in Minneapolis, has worked on half a dozen breweries and more than a hundred restaurants in his career. His brewery experience ranges from tiny Bang Brewing in St. Paul to Surly's massive destination taproom.

Pechman saw a shift in brewery designs after the taproom bill passed. He notes that the breweries were "still a utilitarian facility but had to shift some focus on aesthetics. After all, they were now in direct competition with the very places that sell their products [bars and restaurants]. They had to project themselves as a destination or at least part of a community if they were to have any success."

One of Pechman's projects, the Pryes Brewing taproom on West River Road in Minneapolis,

The Island City Brewing Company taproom in downtown Winona is cozy and open. The eclectic seating makes it feel like your great-aunt's kitchen, while the natural wood and exposed brick reflect the building's industrial qualities.

PRYES BREWING

A CASE STUDY, BY JEREMY NELSON

Pryes Brewing asked Little Box to design its space because of our extensive background with restaurant projects and their desire to be more than just "a garage with some picnic tables." They were serious about masterfully creating craft beer and wanted the taproom to have the same thoughtfulness in design.

Pryes was already distributing beer and creating a following [prior to opening its taproom]. Knowing that this following was there meant a little flexibility on space selection. Several locations were reviewed for pedestrian

The Pryes Brewing Company taproom presents a warm atmosphere and creative design elements within an industrial warehouse structure.

access, vehicle traffic, budget, and space constraints over twelve months. The chosen location at the edge of downtown is able to capture some of the happy hour crowd, provide parking, view the river, and have five areas within the taproom for patrons to find where they're comfortable.

The quality of a space is judged by what is directly experienced; the taste of the beer, light levels, comfortable seating, quality materials within touch range, and amenities all play a role. A wider variety of people are frequenting taprooms, and they may bring with them pets, children, a client for a business meeting, or a large group for a party. Because of this, the taproom needs to be flexible and offer amenities that keep most entertained for an enjoyable experience.

Many times, keeping the space flexible means basic and plain without character, but the design of Pryes keeps the flexibility while also being a distinct and memorable experience. A large item in Pryes is a game: feather bowling, a game kids could play and also something for competition with league play. A few other key features are an extensive patio, grass area for pets, a cluster restroom with unisex stalls, views to the production facility, in-house kitchen, and quality materials and custom furniture made of cold rolled steel, brass, and rich walnut.

Pryes is already quite large at more than 12,000 square feet, but while designing the space there were items built in and thought of for expansion. A mezzanine and/or rooftop space is not out of the question for a future taproom expansion. Little Box also worked with Pryes on the layout and flow of the production space to allow for a possible expansion into the area next to their space in order to accommodate their growing distribution and production needs.

is rife with beautiful features. He was brought in to design the tables, bar top, and tap lines. "The tap tower is something special, though," Pechman says. "There are light cannons behind every tap spout. As you pull the tap, it activates the light and illuminates the beer a wonderfully amber color. I wanted to showcase how clean the beer is and also wanted the thought of the customer getting a glass of pure liquid gold."

Unpretentious but effective features like this are key to Pechman's designs. For him, Restoration Hardware furniture and a window to the brewhouse equipment simply won't cut it. There must be more to the taproom's design than what can be bought and assembled out of a showroom. "Give me an experience and give me a reason to come back," Pechman admonishes. In his own work, he wants a visitor to notice something new with each visit. He says, "The more times you can reward a viewer with a new treat, the better."

The ways in which the design intentions of restaurants and breweries differ is informed by their business goals, according to Pechman. While restaurants aim to turn tables, he says, "taprooms want you to stay and have another." He adds, "A proper restaurant is built with these things in mind: food, service, atmosphere, and libations. A proper taproom, in my humble opinion, should be built with these things in mind: libations, atmosphere, community, and social connectivity. After all, we all want to find a place where everybody knows your name."

Pechman believes that both taprooms and restaurants need to be inviting, but these key differences in the goals and intentions of the spaces will alter the way they are designed. For example, taprooms have plenty of standing room, something a restaurant cannot offer its patrons while they eat dinner. Using standing room allows a taproom to fit more paying patrons in a space and encourages them to engage with one another rather than leaning back in chairs across a table from one another.

I have been to nearly every taproom in Minnesota, which means I've seen just about everything there is to see in taproom designs. Some are pole barns, others reside in strip malls, and still others occupy retrofitted historic buildings. Murals, chalkboard beer menus, local art, and concrete floors are all common features to varying degrees, but each taproom has a unique personality. Pryes is a particularly striking taproom because of the elevated design, including dark wood with gold accents, coupled with classic taproom features like Edison bulbs and communal seating.

Jeremy Nelson, architect and principal of the Minneapolis-based architecture and design firm Little Box, Inc., agrees that taproom design is crucial to a brewery's success. Brewery owners should consider the experience offered by their taprooms nearly as important as the beer they're brewing. "The beer should always come first," asserts Nelson, adding: "After beer, the location, budget, design style, and company mission inform each other."

Reflecting on the influx of taprooms that came with the taproom bill's passage in 2011, Nelson says: "In order to make it in the industry, the [brewery] owners need to decide—long before even looking for a location—what type of taproom they want to open and come to terms with their business plan. Will the brewery be content as a small neighborhood spot tucked in a garage, sharing their creations with local residents and friends? Do they want to join the five percent that manage margins of marketing, restaurant distribution, and canning?"

More than Frozen Pizzas

Any good party needs two things: food and beer. But most brewery owners are in the craft beer industry for the beer, not to run a restaurant. Surprise, I know.

Operating a kitchen out of a taproom requires a brewery owner to procure extra licenses, hire additional staff, and essentially run a second business while continuing to operate their primary venture. A few Minnesota breweries pursue this taproom-plus-restaurant model: Surly, Urban Growler, and Wooden Hill are just a few. Needless to say, it is far easier to run a brewery without having to worry about providing hot food options. However, this setup can leave brewers with progressively drunker patrons who, rather than staying to enjoy another round or two, head elsewhere to grab a bite to eat. The lost revenue is measurable as paying customers walk out the door.

And then, on the second day, the gods gave us food trucks. A symbiotic relationship between food trucks and taprooms began to emerge at the very beginning of the taproom boom. Food trucks started appearing in Minnesota around 2010, and several served at taprooms in their earliest days. The taprooms presented a captive and hungry audience for the food trucks, and food trucks solved the problem of providing sustenance for hungry beer drinkers. You can find food trucks that serve up everything from cheese curds to ramen, vegan tacos to smoky barbecue, and breweries work to bring these mobile food vendors to their taproom doorstep—kind of like an ice cream truck for beer drinkers.

Since the initial boom, new models of the taproom–food truck relationship have emerged. For example, La Doña Cervecería, LynLake Brewery, and Pryes Brewing in Minneapolis built permanent kitchens within their taprooms that serve as host to a rotating roster of pop-up restaurants. The responsibility of running the kitchen is off the brewery's back, but the taproom still reaps the benefits of offering food to patrons, enticing them to stay longer and, hopefully, buy more beer.

Fulton Brewing took a different approach with its Minneapolis taproom. The brewery developed a permanent food truck that was physically separate from the brewery but remained on-site. Like the permanent kitchen model, the brewery-owned food truck model ensures regular food offerings for patrons without being at the mercy of icy roads or broken generators or other restrictions that can hamper traditional food trucks. Although this approach sacrifices the variety and partnerships offered by relationships with rotating food trucks, these breweries gain consistency and a committed revenue stream.

Fulton, which was the first brewery to open a taproom in Minneapolis following the passage of the taproom bill, has also adapted to the changing nature of food trucks and their relationships with taprooms. Tucker Gerrick, Fulton's marketing director, recalls the early days of their food service. At the time, food trucks were

La Doña Cervecería is similar to other Minnesota taprooms in many ways, although the built-in kitchen helps to set it apart. On weekends, salsa dancers take over a side room at the brewery.

gaining popularity and, Gerrick says, "it was extremely beneficial to have and host a variety of food trucks on our premises." But as time went on and the Fulton business evolved, they saw that bringing the food experience in-house was a way for the brewery to control its brand more and to use food as a marketing opportunity. "Of course, extra sales is always good for the bottom line," Gerrick adds, "but thinking more long term, it made sense to begin serving our own food as it allowed us to tell the Fulton story more broadly." In 2017, Fulton refurbished a 1969 Airstream Land Yacht to function as the taproom kitchen, with executive chef Scott Pampuch serving up familiar pub fare. In 2020, as the taproom was expanding with a major construction project, the food offerings changed along with it. Nikole Harris, the taproom general manager, says, "The future of Fulton Taproom's food experience will include a very approachable, fun, and affordable menu." The taproom will also explore offering lunch and to-go programs with the goal of connecting not just with taproom patrons but also with people who live and work in the North Loop neighborhood. Fulton's model shows the potential for multiple types of food service in a taproom, each offering benefits as well as challenges as a brewery grows and changes.

Dogs

Much of craft beer culture dictates that if you visit a taproom, you are almost guaranteed the opportunity to pet at least one pooch and dub them a very good dog. Taprooms offer some of the few public venues where dogs are welcome indoors, not to mention the plethora of dog-friendly patios. Before taprooms, the options for dog-friendly social gatherings consisted of public parks and—well, that's about it.

Groups such as Sidewalk Dog host community events at dog-friendly taprooms, and dog owners have been known to host doggie birthday parties and meetups in taprooms. Ali Jarvis of Sidewalk Dog says, "There are not a lot of options in Minnesota, where we have cold winters and short summers. Breweries are the only option for a lot of people who don't have money to go to day cares or something like that. From a design perspective, breweries are not carpeted and tend to have a lot of space between tables. They tend to have benches that won't tip over like chairs will, and not every table has food on it driving your dog crazy."

Casey Matter, also of Sidewalk Dog, points out that the demographics of dog people and brewery-goers often overlap—they are under thirty-five years old, have disposable income, and oftentimes don't have kids. Both craft beer drinkers and dog owners are looking for social communities, and breweries serve as an ideal space to bring together those two passions.

However, just as brewers had to fight for the right to brew and pour beer in their own taprooms, breweries in Minneapolis also had to fight for the right to allow dogs inside their spaces. While many taprooms quietly allowed dogs inside before it was legal, a new city ordinance in May 2017 permitted dogs inside Minneapolis taprooms, as long as

Dogs are a familiar sight at many Minnesota taprooms, both inside and out.

SUPPORTING NONPROFITS

Part of being a member of a community is giving back through charitable work and donations, and taprooms are no exception to that principle. Many taprooms host charitable-giving nights where they arrange to donate a portion of their proceeds to a specific charity. In the case of Indeed Brewing, 100 percent of the proceeds every Wednesday benefit a charity selected by employees. The program, Indeed We Can, generates $70,000 to $80,000 annually for local nonprofits. Many other breweries host regular charitable-giving days or donate their spaces to nonprofit partners.

they (the breweries, not the dogs) apply for and receive a variance. Like all things involving beer, there are rules and regulations attached—taprooms that choose to be dog friendly cannot also operate an indoor kitchen—but it was a big win for dog-owning city dwellers and beer field trip takers who plan to spend the day on the town with their pooches, contributing to both the local economy and their taste buds.

BEER FESTIVALS

Beer festivals can be raucous displays of debauchery by several hundred grown-ass adults. They are also a place for people to enjoy craft beer in community while sampling the best that breweries have to offer. Without having to drive all over the state, festival attendees can learn about breweries near and far. In return, the breweries connect with potential new customers who may never have been exposed to their beers before.

A festival might be unique in its focus: winter seasonals, quirky infusions, or style invitationals. It might feature great local music and entertainment. Or it might just aim to bring a wide variety of beer to the community. Regardless, the day's events usually unfold in a similar manner. Dozens of breweries set up tents and jockey boxes (repurposed coolers with tap lines linked to kegs under the table) in neat lines around a festival ground, which can be anything from a parking lot to a city park to a convention center. Visitors take their four-ounce sample cups from brewer to brewer and back again to get a taste of each one's flagship beers and specialty releases.

In 1982, the beer festival that begins and ends all modern American beer festivals was born: the Great American Beer Festival (GABF). Held annually in Colorado, GABF is another beloved brainchild of industry legend Charlie Papazian. It started with 22 participating breweries and 800 attendees in 1982. In 2019, GABF boasted 800 breweries in attendance; more than 4,000 different beers from nearly 2,300 breweries representing all 50 states and the District of Columbia; and 60,000 attendees.

If a beer lover were so inclined, they could find themselves at a beer festival in Minnesota on just about every weekend during the summer. From municipal fests to more exclusive experiences, there is no shortage of organized beer drinking in Minnesota. Following are a few festivals worth noting.

Beer Dabbler Festivals

The Beer Dabbler is the parent company behind Minnesota's now shuttered premier craft beer publication *The Growler*. It hosts three annual festivals that typically feature trendy and creative beers. A brewery might bring its regular crowd-pleasers, but the festivals are an opportunity to show off a brewer's creativity with infused beers and special limited releases.

Summer Dabbler takes place in the heat of August, most recently at CHS Field in St. Paul. Founded in 2009, the festival now features more than 140 breweries sampling more than 450 beers.

Winter Dabbler is a snow-covered February expedition at the state fairgrounds. The festival was founded in 2010 and now welcomes more than 180 breweries and cideries pouring more than 600 beers and ciders. Joe Alton, then editor of *The Growler*, told the magazine in 2017, "There are 364 other days in the year to obsess over the nuances of your beer. ... An outdoor beer festival in Minnesota in February is an opportunity to have fun and celebrate our spirit of the northern hardiness together."

Pride Dabbler is a glitter-infused extravaganza with live music and plenty of food trucks in Minneapolis's Loring Park. It's part of the Twin Cities Pride Festival, which celebrates the LGBTQ+ community in Minnesota. The 2012-founded beer festival originally connected dozens of Minnesota breweries with food trucks to create food and beer pairings. Now it encourages those breweries to pull out all the stops to best play off the assigned brewery theme that year. Themes have included Lady Gaga, drag queens, and LGBTQ+ icons. To say breweries go all out for Pride Dabbler is an understatement: you'll find body glitter, beer glitter, costumes, temporary tattoos, build-your-own-infusions, Britney Spears flights, and a whole lot of good fun.

The Winter Beer Dabbler requires a hardy spirit and thick gloves and boots.

Plus, participating breweries can choose to donate the stipend they receive for their beer to a scholarship fund established by the Beer Dabbler. The scholarship, titled Pride in Brewing, benefits LGBTQ+ beer students at Dakota County Technical College.

Minnesota Craft Brewers Guild Festivals

As the professional association for Minnesota brewers, the Minnesota Craft Brewers Guild (MNCBG) hosts three annual festivals to raise funds for the organization, while fostering a stronger brewing community and celebrating great beer in the process. These are the fests where breweries pour to impress—beers are specially selected with the knowledge that industry professionals will be tasting alongside the "civilian" attendees.

All Pints North is a summer celebration of Minnesota beer hosted on the shores of Lake Superior at Bayfront Festival Park in Duluth. The festival, started in 2012, features live music, food, and a giant party. It has become an industry favorite because it offers the chance to show off great summer brews while partying in the sunshine at a beautiful up-north destination. A brewer described it to Lauren Bennett McGinty, executive director of the MNCBG, as a "brewer's vacation." The festival was open to regional brewers until 2018, when it became restricted to members of the Minnesota Craft Brewers Guild. It's a feat for a festival of that size—with 110 breweries pouring that year—to feature exclusively Minnesota brands. Such a task would have been impossible just a few years earlier.

Autumn Brew Review was founded in 2001 as an outdoor regional beer festival. Bennett McGinty recalls it being "teeny tiny," with few attendees and a handful of brewers pouring. The festival moved around Minneapolis to different venues over the years as it grew. At first, Autumn Brew Review was a kickoff to the colder months and the heavier beers that come with the change in seasons. "For a really long time," Bennett McGinty says, "there was a super big emphasis on everybody releasing their specialty winter and fall beers, which was always such a big deal." She recalls in particular the early years of seeking out Fitger's special releases that weren't available anywhere outside of the brewery's Duluth taproom. Since then, the festival has grown beyond a small gathering featuring big beers poured by the folks who brewed them.

The festival has shifted in other ways, too. It got pushed from September to October because, with the effects of climate change, September became too hot for a festival rife with dark beers for the fall and winter seasons. The number of brewers pouring at the Autumn Brew review also increased significantly, in part due to the growing number of brewers but also due to changing consumer expectations. Bennett McGinty says, "Unfortunately you can't sell tickets for ten breweries bringing their most amazing, barrel-aged beers anymore because the newest craft beer drinkers probably have no idea what that even is." These days, ABR hosts more than one hundred Minnesota breweries and cideries alongside food and live music on the banks of the Mississippi.

Winterfest is a higher-end festival that allows craft beer fans to enjoy the beers they love along with specially designed small-plate dishes. Highlighting the state's craft beer as well as its top chefs, the impact is similar to that of the craft beer dinners that once reigned. Further elevating the experience of Winterfest, breweries have collaborated with restaurants to create exclusive specialty beers to complement the food offerings. In 2018, for example, Brasa Rotisserie was partnered with four Minneapolis breweries: Able, Fair State, 612Brew, and Bauhaus. The restaurant created a single dish with which each of its partner breweries paired two beers. Able paired its Easy Tiger Pale Ale with Brasa's citrus-glazed smoked pork over tostones, garnished with ginger crema and pickled onions. The exact configuration of food and beer pairings has changed over the years since the festival's inception, but the results are always mouthwatering.

Winterfest, founded in 2002, has also shifted locations as it has grown: from the Landmark Center and Union Depot in St. Paul to the Target Center in Minneapolis. In January 2020, it was held at U.S. Bank Stadium, with more than one hundred Minnesota breweries pouring.

The possibilities around the beer-food pairings excite Bennett McGinty. For a long time, she says, craft beer was about the craziest things you could do to a beer. Kumquat beer? Why not? That came at the cost, however, of allowing wine to remain the champion beverage for food pairing. Bennett McGinty says that now Winterfest is about showing food, beer, and wine lovers alike just what a craft beer is capable of doing for your palate. Plus, she adds, the fest has helped to elevate local food as well as beer.

Brewery-Hosted Festivals

While industry pros and craft beer aficionados attend Beer Dabbler and MNCBG festivals in droves, there are a few brewery-hosted festivals that have become favorites as well.

Junkyard Brewing Company has hosted its Rare Beer Picnic in Moorhead every summer since 2015. Junkyard invites Minnesota and out-of-state breweries to pour their best aged, soured, and infused beers at a festival featuring live music and great food.

Since 2016, Fair State in Minneapolis has hosted Mixed Culture, where the brewery shows off its own funky and sour beers alongside those of a few collaborators.

In May 2019, Forager and Little Thistle Breweries in Rochester hosted the first Gathering in the Wood festival, which invites select brewers from Minnesota and beyond to pour beer that has been aged or fermented in wood.

Lupulin Brewing in Big Lake launched its IPA Invitational in the summer of 2018. Twenty-three breweries attended the inaugural festival with the best of their best IPAs. In 2019, the IPA Invitational featured twenty-seven breweries, about half from Minnesota and half out-of-staters who introduced their beers to Minnesota's hop-loving population.

In addition to hosting gatherings that bring together breweries from around the state or region, many breweries throw parties for reasons other than sampling a wide variety of beers. Entertainment often includes concerts, food trucks, local craftspeople, and beer releases. More niche gatherings might include roller-skating (Modist), Skateboard Olympics (Bauhaus), and a harvest festival (Lakes and Legends).

THE BREWING PROCESS

The communities and third places created as a result of the craft beer industry in Minnesota would be nothing without its driving force: the beer. In most Minnesota taprooms, the brewing equipment is visible from your barstool. While state law requires a brewhouse to be immediately adjacent to its respective taproom, brewery owners often leave the brewing equipment out in the open or visible behind large windows as a way to underscore the transparent nature of the craft. The process is laid bare for you to witness, and that is a major draw—it connects consumers with their breweries while offering a behind-the-scenes look at how their beer is made.

Brewing systems are usually constructed of stainless steel vessels purchased from a variety of national and international sources. Some may be picked up used from another brewery. A typical brewhouse will also have dry storage for malted barley, cold storage for pelletized hops, and a laboratory space for quality control.

Minnesota's breweries boast systems ranging from one barrel (31 gallons) to 150 barrels and an even greater range of fermentation systems. Your neighborhood taproom's system is likely somewhere in the range of seven barrels.

The first vessel used in the brewing process is the mash tun. Here, malted barley and other cereal grains are mixed with hot water. The amount and variety of malts used plus the temperature of the water fundamentally determine the beer that ends up in your pint glass. At the end of this hour-plus-long mixing process, naturally occurring enzymes in the grains have converted long sugar chains into shorter,

Where the magic happens: the brewhouse. Imminent Brewing's brewhouse in Northfield is full of stainless steel equipment.

more fermentable ones to produce a sweet liquid called wort. The leftover barley hulls from the mash tun are often given to farmers for livestock feed, relieving the brewery of any disposal fees.

The wort is then transferred to the boil kettle, the next vessel in the brewing process. True to its name, the boil kettle brings the wort up to a boil for around an hour, killing off microorganisms. Boiling also helps evaporate precursors for off flavors such as dimethyl sulfide. Brewers also add a variety of hop pellets to the boil kettle at set times to introduce new flavors and, sometimes, bitterness to the brew. If the brewer has a whirlpool tank, hops are added there rather than in the boil kettle.

Hop cones grow as soft green buds on bines and are harvested in autumn. (A bine plant climbs by wrapping its stem in a helix around a supporting structure, rather than using tendrils as a vine would.) The vast farms where hops grow look almost like vineyards, but the product smells way better. Most brewers purchase their hops from

Whole hop cones grown on the patio at Forager Brewery.

specific regions of the country where soil and climate are ideal for producing great flavors. Hops' leafy exteriors are particularly messy for brewers, so their juicy, lupulin-filled innards are usually pelletized and then vacuum sealed for shelf stability. In the fall, around the time of the hop harvest, some breweries use fresh hops straight from the bine in the brewing process. The result is called a fresh- or wet-hopped beer, and it is packed with dank flavors and aromas.

In our IPA-crazed beer culture, I would be remiss to not share with you the glory of hops. Just as certain malts can produce light pilsners and roasty porters, hops can impart flavors of stone fruits, pine, citrus, and grassiness.

Hops are usually the only ingredient added in the whirlpool stage of the process—whether in a boil kettle or whirlpool tank—but a range of other ingredients can be mixed in to bring unique flavors to the beer. Zested lemons or oak chips tied up in a makeshift tea bag might be added, or lactobacillus bacteria may be used to create a kettle sour. Don't be grossed out by the bacteria: just think of it like sourdough bread, except you probably shouldn't have the resulting product for breakfast.

The super hot liquid from the boil kettle is then cooled down and

BARREL PROGRAMS

We can map out the brewing process until my face turns blue, but I will never write enough pages to explain the nuances of chemistry and creativity that make each beer in Minnesota possible. That's especially true when it comes to barrel programs.

Beer can be transferred from multiple stages in the brewing process into barrels that are ripe with wine, whiskey, bourbon, or even tequila. Often these barrels are purchased from distillers or wineries for their rich flavors. In these barrels, a beer will either ferment or age, taking on an often unpredictable shape of its own.

Barrel programs can be expensive, they take up significant real estate in a brewery, and they're not guaranteed to produce the result you're looking for. That being said, they are a brewer's playground and a beer geek's paradise, so they live on as passion projects while other beers pay the bills.

Barrel racks tower high in the Lupulin Brewing Company brewhouse in Big Lake.

Co-owners Erin Hutton, Becka Giesen, and Tom Giesen of Giesenbräu Bier Co. sample some of the brewery's products straight out of the tank. Giesenbräu is a family-owned and -operated brewery based in New Prague.

transferred to temperature-controlled fermenters (all those tanks you see with cone-shaped bottoms). Usually those fermenters are chilled with a double-walled jacket of glycol, which is a big step up from the caves we used to rely on to keep things cold. For each beer, specific yeast strains are selected to chomp down on all the sugar from the wort, and the temperature of the fermenter is set to whatever is ideal for that yeast as well as the beer style.

With all those organisms going to town at their personal Old Country Buffet, we end up with two by-products: alcohol and carbon dioxide. The CO2 is released from the fermenters via a simple tube submerged in a bucket of sanitizer (cheap vodka will also do the trick), which lets bubbles out and keeps anything dirty from coming in. The alcohol stays in. Once the yeast is done doing its work, brewers harvest it from the fermenter to reuse in another round of fermenting.

The fermentation vessel is also where the dry-hopping process occurs. Adding hop pellets to the fermented beer transmits pungent hop flavors and aromas to the beer without increasing its bitterness. Dry hop pellets can be added days apart after fermentation ends, sometimes several times, to add to the hop profile and intensity.

Now that we have full-fledged beer on our hands, the final liquid typically gets filtered—though sometimes not, which leaves you with floaties and flavors—and transferred to the brite tank, the final vessel in the brewing process, from which cans and kegs are filled. In the brite tank, the beer is artificially injected with controlled CO_2 to achieve ideal carbonation.

And, dear reader, that's how you get beer. Well, that's one way to get beer. Artistic and scientific brewers are always finding new (and old) ways to tweak the process and create new flavor experiences.

MINNESOTA CRAFT BREWERIES

SIXTEEN PROFILES

The stories of Minnesota craft beer are best illustrated by its brewers. Each brewery and taproom tells the tales of growth, community, business, and identity. Their teams range from a ragtag bunch of garage brewers figuring it out as they go to highly trained professionals with formal educations in microbiology, chemistry, and brewing. The brewery's events become your block parties, and their taproom your neighborhood gathering place. Minnesota's craft breweries are undeniably embedded in our communities and culture.

What follows is a series of profiles that highlights a handful of Minnesota breweries. These breweries are some of the largest, the oldest, the most influential, or simply my favorites in Minnesota. While these case studies do not tell the story of every brewer in Minnesota—far from it, in fact—they paint a picture of how Minnesota craft beer has grown to become the fixture it is today.

Each brewery profile begins with some basic data, such as the year the brewery opened, its barrel production as reported by the Brewers Association, and key members of the team, emphasizing those who contributed to the book with interviews and other insights. Following an overview of the brewery's story are lists of the key beers you should know and the major awards the brewery has won. These last two categories of information are not exhaustive, and the beers mentioned are simply those that I and/or the brewery owners feel you should know about. I worked with representatives from each brewery to select which brews to highlight, and I relied on the brewery's own descriptions of the beer. The beers might be the major flagship offerings that we all know and love, or they may be the rare specialty releases that are not large in volume but are meaningful to the brewery and its fans. The award sections focus on the more significant honors for the beers themselves, such as the coveted medals awarded at the annual Great American Beer Festival. Most of these breweries have also received a wide range of accolades above and beyond their beer—such as for community service, business and entrepreneurship, design, or even best beertender tattoos. Even if they are not listed here, such accolades are meaningful indications of a brewery's contributions to Minnesota and its craft beer communities.

SUMMIT BREWING COMPANY

A TRUE LEADER AND PIONEER IN MINNESOTA CRAFT BEER

St. Paul, Minnesota
Brewery opened: 1986
Beer hall opened: 2013
Barrels produced (2019): 128,000; largest in state by production
The Team: Mark Stutrud, founder and president

THE EARLY DAYS

It's impossible to talk about—or drink—Minnesota beer without addressing Mark Stutrud and his brewery. Summit Brewing Company, founded in 1986, is a staple in nearly every bar and beer fridge in Minnesota. Summit Extra Pale Ale is a consistent, easy choice on any beer menu, and the brewery's themed mix packs showcase the variety it offers within the company's philosophy of tradition and balance.

In 2019, the brewery's thirty-third year of operation, Summit surpassed August Schell Brewing Company as the largest brewery by production in Minnesota, pumping out 128,000 barrels to Schell's 117,300. For drinkers like me who weren't around to witness Summit's beginnings, the brewery seems like an invincible paragon

Summit founder Mark Stutrud posed inside a brew kettle shortly after opening his new brewery facility along the Mississippi River in St. Paul. *Photo courtesy of Summit Brewing*

of craft beer. In my mind, Summit has simply always existed and always will. History, however, reveals a more tumultuous story about Summit Brewing Company.

Before starting his own brewery, Mark Stutrud left his social work profession after years in the chemical dependency field. Unsure what his next step would be, he asked, *Well, what the hell am I going to do with myself?* This attitude carried Stutrud through the next several decades: hard work and a dose of humble humor. His homebrewing hobby—and remember, homebrewing only became legal in Minnesota in 1985—led him to investigate what the "brave souls" who were opening breweries elsewhere in the country in the eighties were up to. He noticed the void created by big beer and thought he might take advantage of it. "With the consolidation of the brewing industry since the sixties and reliance on mass volumes of a singular type of beer, [large breweries] literally created opportunities for the resurgence of small-scale brewing or microbreweries or craft brewing, whatever you want to call it," says Stutrud.

SUMMIT BY THE NUMBERS

Located off a business access road along the Mississippi River, St. Paul's Summit Brewing is in an expansive facility. The two buildings from which Summit operates encompass 112,500 square feet. Here's a breakdown of the square footage:

Brewhouse: 25,000 square feet
Fermentation: 25,000 square feet
Packaging (bottling, canning, kegging): 20,000 square feet
Warehouse: 15,000 square feet
Cold storage: 15,000 square feet
Office space: 10,000 square feet
Ratskeller (beer hall): 2,500 square feet

The opportunity for a successful craft brewery in Minnesota was clearly present, but Stutrud wasn't one to jump in without doing his research. While craft beer enjoyed a resurgence in the eighties, it was still early in the trend. Plus, opening a brewery in 1980s Minnesota meant spending all your energy on production and distribution—without the option for alternative revenue streams from a taproom or growler sales.

Stutrud spent a couple of years using up his vacation time at work to research breweries around the country. His list included Redhook Brewery in Seattle and the now-defunct Newman Brewing in Albany. He also met many professionals in the beer industry who would become mentors and advisors. In this time, Stutrud earned his degree from the Siebel Institute, one of the most respected institutions in the world for training craft brewers.

Finally, in 1984, Stutrud began working on his own brewery full time. He recounts, "I knew that we needed to be technically focused and technically sound because we were confronted immediately with competing head-on with all the major brewers." At the time, Stutrud says, the beer scene was relatively homogenous. For example, only a few bars in St. Paul—a city that prides itself on its Irish heritage—had Guinness on tap. Anchor Steam was sprinkled across the Twin Cities, and Sam Adams and Sierra Nevada weren't even on the scene yet. "There were no other small breweries in the area," Stutrud continues. "Back then, we were not only busting sod and cultivating the notion of what we were up to; we were also selling and delivering our own beer."

It is a small miracle that the brewery survived its first few years, given that not a single distributor would consider touching Summit with a ten-foot pole. In the first year, Stutrud says, "They wouldn't even talk to us, let alone sit down and have a beer."

But once distributors realized Summit wasn't going anywhere and might be a potential distribution client, conversations between the two entities finally began. If the distributors couldn't beat the little upstart brewer that was stealing away their tap lines, they had to join him.

BREWING THE CLASSICS

There are plenty of people in the craft beer community who would call Mark Stutrud old school. To that he responds, "Shit, thanks for noticing." You have to appreciate a guy who says what he's thinking.

Stutrud continues: "I love it when people criticize me for being classical and traditional—that's who we are. Yeah, we have fun with different styles, but we're purists and we're also fanatics about being technically proper. For us to come out with a new style, it's about six to twelve months' worth of work, and sometimes more."

What goes into all that work? It starts with a dedicated team, which consists of Damian McConn, a supremely qualified head brewer with experience at Guinness, and seven brewers working under him; a team of five quality control staff, including microbiologists

The massive size of Summit Brewing's equipment would make any homebrewer's jaw drop.
Photo courtesy of Summit Brewing

and chemists; and plenty of ears and eyes—and taste buds—on the market, ranging from beer hall patrons to retailers and all the way up to distributors. Each beer is meticulously researched, tested, brewed, analyzed, and reviewed.

You don't get to be the largest brewery in the state without a certain level of professional rigor, and Stutrud believes it should exist in all brewers. "There is this element of homebrewers who want to go pro," he says, "but one of the things that they lack is the training and the discipline of how a professional brewer thinks. A professional brewer is no different than a professional musician. When it comes to composition, you have the melody, you've got that musical notion in your mind, and you've got a pretty definite idea of what it is you're going to put together that's translated into a score or an orchestration, which is no different than a formulation [for a beer]."

"You have all that stuff down in black and white," Stutrud continues. "Not just the ingredients, but the process steps and everything else before you get people together to rehearse. And when you're rehearsing, you're perfecting. You're not smoking a joint and saying, 'Jeez, this feels really good. I think I'm just going to throw these things together and see what happens.' That is not professional brewing. That's more of a homebrewer."

A former homebrewer himself, Stutrud isn't disparaging homebrewers with that comment. Rather, with the proliferation of amateurs entering the brewing industry in the wake of the 2011 taproom bill, he is emphasizing the need for homebrewers to "up their game" before attempting to make the transition to commercial brewer. It's a word of caution to folks looking to get into the industry: mediocre won't cut it.

Stutrud did not take the task of starting a brewery lightly. His goal, he says, was to "reincorporate a true beer culture in our society." This means his focus was—and still is—on imparting a solid understanding of "the classics" in consumers so they might use that knowledge as a foundation for dialogue about beer styles and flavors. Prohibition, according to Stutrud, had wiped out any appreciation or knowledge our culture had for beer styles and how they stemmed from unique societies and seasons. He wants consumers to ask questions like, *What is the origin of this malt? Why is that yeast used for a certain style of beer? Whose ancestors developed this recipe—when and where did they brew it?* Everything Summit produces is Stutrud's response to this lack of awareness in American beer drinkers. "It truly is a reeducation process," he says. "I just didn't think that it was going to take this long."

ON CONSISTENCY

This probably goes without saying, but something about how Summit (and Mark Stutrud) operates achieves one maxim more clearly than others can or do: a brewery should be built on consistent, quality beer. To brew quality beer, a brewer must be doing quality work. Stutrud puts it plainly: "Quality just doesn't happen. It's predetermined" by the efforts of the brewer.

And consistent quality is something Summit is known for. If you fell in love with Summit EPA twenty years ago, you can drink and get the same enjoyment out of that brew today—and at just about any bar

Precision and focus at all stages of the brewing process reinforce Summit's high standards of reliability and consistency. *Photo courtesy of Summit Brewing*

in the state, to boot. Summit's scrupulous attention to consistency and quality in its brewing ensures a product that endures the tests of time and taste. This feat is one not many brewers at the time could boast, and it's a trait Stutrud openly admires in the big brewers like Anheuser-Busch and Miller. It's also a skill that ultimately separates the wheat from the chaff.

For a while, Summit's reputation for reliability struck the wrong chord with Stutrud. It read to him as expected and unexciting. He explains, "The hair would stand up on the back of my neck when somebody said, 'You're my go-to beer or my standby.'" But when he listened closer, he heard something different: consumers saw Summit as a benchmark by which to measure other beers.

Stutrud says, "It's fun to sit down with somebody who hasn't had an EPA for five years and they go, 'Holy shit, this is great.'" He focuses on brewing recipes that are drinkable and balanced, and he appreciates a beer drinker coming back to his now-classic brews to discover their technical value and overall balance. In Stutrud's world, balance means the four ingredients of beer—water, malt, hops, and yeast—all work together rather than one dominating the flavor. In a drinking culture crazed with hop-bombs and lactose-sweetened brews, Stutrud's style is not a trendy one, but he thinks it will last. "It's not that I don't like hops," he says. "I like hops a lot. I just don't want the hops to dominate the entire experience in my mind. That's just as linear as drinking a Miller Lite." And he aims to be anything but linear.

There have never been more breweries operating in America than there are right now. Yet, for the first time ever, beer is losing significant market share to spirits and wine. "There have never been more choices. Sadly, there's [also] never been more substandard beer," says Stutrud.

As the market is inundated with new breweries, styles, and releases, many brewers believe consumers behave like moths to a flame: attracted to the brightest, shiniest object in the room. Whatever beer is fresh, flashy, or hyped on Instagram will be what they purchase. But Stutrud believes we are on the precipice of a shift in taste: "I think consumers—even quite a few of the younger drinkers—are starting to get fatigued with exploration. They're getting a little bit impatient with inconsistency, or they'll have a beer that was really cool and nice tasting, and then the next time they tried it, it was wildly different." He expects the constant beer chasing eventually will give way to an appreciation for ol' reliable, and consumer tolerance for inconsistency or even outright mistakes by brewers will diminish.

Stutrud believes that, amidst the flurry of new breweries that have opened in recent years, brewers have been able to get away with releasing brewhouse science experiments as new beer. Even if the brewer knows the experiment may have failed to meet their expectations, they are reluctant to pour a batch of expensive ingredients down the drain, so they put it on tap and hope it sells. And if it tastes good, then who cares if the beer is unbalanced or extreme? To Stutrud, this may be the cardinal sin of brewing. "This blind experimentation is projected and marketed as innovation," he says.

And, he adds, he could never have gotten away with that when Summit was getting started: "In 1986, we would have had our asses thrown out." But he's also lightening up a bit, too: "It used to piss me off, but if I'm not going to take myself too seriously, I've got to ease up a little bit on my attitude."

Attitude or not, Stutrud is right: experimentation is a key component of the ever-evolving craft beer world. More so than in many other industries, consumers are willing to offer themselves up as guinea pigs for brewers' experimentation and also for their own learning curves, according to Stutrud. Why are consumers willing to give so many new breweries a shot and stick with them through their exploratory periods? Maybe it's because we see the brewery as our neighbor and a familiar friend. Maybe it's because we know craft brewers are the underdog, and it feels good to support a local business and a dream.

Mark Stutrud surveys an endless field of barley—"the soul of beer." *Photo courtesy of Summit Brewing*

For Stutrud, creating a consistent brand comes down to the business plan: "There are some folks who are less concerned about establishing a flagship or being known for something. And they are known for creating a new beer every week or every month. That's in efforts to satiate the appetite of the adventurous, experimental, promiscuous drinker who's always looking for something new."

Although he believes the exploration process for new brewers and drinkers is natural, it leaves brewers in a predicament. Put simply, "it's just not sustainable." New recipe development, new spaces on liquor store shelves, new tap lines, new brew day routines to nail down—one business can handle only so many product launches in a year. In Stutrud's world, perfecting a quality flagship outvalues innovation for innovation's sake: "There is very strong evidence of people returning to the classics. That gives Summit a very, very strong position to not only compete but to thrive, because that's what we're known for." According to Nielsen data, while IPAs still dominate the craft beer sector in terms of volume production, the American lager style saw a 50 percent increase in dollars spent in 2019 and pilsners experienced a 23 percent increase.

PUTTING THE CRAFT IN CRAFT BEER

Summit is known for its old-world styles and traditional underpinnings, but that doesn't mean the brewery isn't "crafty." In fact, Summit has taken the spirits of collaboration, local sourcing, and attentive brewing and made them their own.

Take Dakota Soul, for example. The traditional, Czech-style pilsener was introduced in January 2018 and features barley grown next door in North Dakota by Stutrud's very own cousins. Their family single-handedly resurrected the barley variety Moravian 37, keeping alive its old-world flavor characteristics for all us drinkers to enjoy. Leave it to a craft brewer to talk about his ingredients like this: "Water is a beer's foundation. Hop is like a spice. Yeast provides the character. But barley—barley is the soul of beer."

Then you have Summit's fermentation techniques. Since the brewery's inception in 1986, it has relied on natural carbonation.

That means Summit keeps the yeast by-product to carbonate the beer rather than fermenting it flat and force carbonating it in a more controlled fashion. Stutrud explains in classic Stutrud fashion: "It's rarely practiced because it's a pain in the ass." The process requires expensive certified pressure vessels and extra careful attention during fermentation, but he believes the results are worth it. With natural carbonation, the beer has tinier bubbles that are softer on the palate, and the drinker will notice subtle aromatics that are otherwise lost.

Despite its being a pain in the ass, Stutrud says the process doesn't have to be all that hard: "If you know what you're doing and if you're connecting all the dots and all the other pieces of the process and staying focused on the health of the yeast, it's just work. That's all it is, is working."

RATSKELLER AND TAPROOMS

For several years following the passage of the taproom bill, Summit chose to not add a taproom to its St. Paul brewery. While new breweries with taprooms were opening left and right, Summit stood its ground. For other brewers, Stutrud says, a taproom provides an opportunity for prospective brewery owners to discover what a brewer's lifestyle and work are all about without investing in distribution and packaging. But for the well-established Summit, operating without a taproom was treating them just fine, and the business model didn't rely on that source of income. Nowadays, I doubt a Minnesotan could name a successful brewery that doesn't have a taproom.

Summit did open a space in 2013 where the public could enjoy pints of beer on Friday nights, but Stutrud admits it resembled a "Lutheran church basement" more than a taproom. It served as a catch-all space: staff lunchroom by day, host to nonprofit events in the evenings, and a meetup space for the free weekend tours. After a few years, as the taproom revolution went on around them at breweries across Minnesota, Stutrud and Summit finally decided to make the leap to a more refined and comfortable taproom space. Staying on-brand for the old-school brewery, in July 2018, Summit opened its old-world version of a taproom: the Ratskeller, which comes from the German word for a bar located in the basement of a city hall.

The new space—a gorgeous 2,500 square feet with a floor-to-ceiling window view of a copper brew kettle—is set up in the style of a German beer hall. As with the beer poured and consumed there, balance is a priority in the Ratskeller. Rather than opening up a full seven days a week and kicking out the nonprofits that relied on the space, Summit keeps the Ratskeller closed to the public on Mondays through Wednesdays so that it is still available to nonprofits.

While Stutrud is looking out for his nonprofit partners, he's taking into account his retail ones as well. In addition to offering a space where Summit lovers can enjoy their favorite beers at the massive production facility, Stutrud also hopes the taproom experience will launch

The Ratskeller—a big improvement on Summit's previous "church basement" tasting room—awaits its afternoon guests.

Summit Extra Pale Ale is a gold standard of Minnesota craft beer.

consumers into a newfound loyalty to Summit wherever they go: "When people come to visit, we want to have them truly have a great time and then leave with that experience and think about it when they patronize their spots."

BEERS TO KNOW

Extra Pale Ale: "A pioneer in craft beer (hey, that rhymes), Summit Extra Pale Ale has been gracing the pint glasses of serious beer lovers since 1986. Bronze color. Gold medal–winning flavor. Featuring caramel, biscuity malts balanced by an earthy hop bite and juicy citrus." 5.1% ABV, 49 IBU

Dakota Soul Craft Lager: "There'd be no Summit Dakota Soul craft lager without the Moravian 37 barley grown exclusively by our founder's cousins near Rugby, North Dakota. Crafted from farm to finish right here in Grain Country, this traditional Czech-style pilsener features notes of English biscuits, honey, and graham cracker, plus a floral, spicy hop finish thanks to genuine Saaz hops and the new American hop variety Loral." 4.8% ABV, 28 IBU

Great Northern Porter: "Originally named after the London market workers who popularized this brew, we dubbed our porter with a nod toward the majestic railway stretching from St. Paul to Seattle. Roasted malts offer up coffee notes and lead to a slightly sweet, chocolatey finish. All aboard!" 5.4% ABV, 51 IBU

Keller Pils: "Brewed with traditional Tettnang hops and the modern German variety Huell Melon, Keller Pils offers spicy floral notes, balanced citrus bitterness, and malty-sweet and honey undertones from Weyermann Barke Pilsner Malt." 5.1% ABV, 38 IBU

Oatmeal Stout: "A beautiful cascade and rich black color familiar to the stout style, Summit Oatmeal Stout is decidedly different. It is brewed with naked oats from the United Kingdom and it is only served on nitro draught. Smooth and slightly sweet, Oatmeal Stout offers hints of coffee, caramel, and chocolate with a creamy finish. A taste you won't find just anywhere." 5.2% ABV, 41 IBU

Sága IPA: "Named after the Norse goddess Sága, drinking companion of the god Odin. Featuring a divine tropical fruit hop aroma and clean, assertive bitterness." 6.3% ABV, 65 IBU

Slugfest Juicy IPA: "Summit Slugfest is an unfiltered IPA with an orange appearance, low in alcohol and bitterness but big in citrus hop flavors and aromas. Seeking to connect new American IPA trends with our classical European approach to brewing, Slugfest offers aggressive and powerful citrus hop flavors and aromas of tangerine, melon, and lemon, thanks to hop varieties Huell Melon, Azacca, and Mandarina Bavaria. Malt notes of toast, English biscuits, and breadcrust. Highly Drinkable. Undeniably Repeatable." 4.7% ABV, 38 IBU

Triumphant Session IPA: "All of the flavor with none of the guilt, Summit Triumphant is for celebrating everyday accomplishments. Hopped in flavor, but not calories or carbs. ... With tropical notes of pineapple, grapefruit, and apricot and balanced bitterness, this brew has all the taste of a traditional IPA at a fraction of the typical IPA ABV. Flavors of breadcrust and sweet citrus lead to a clean, bitter finish. It is the Beer for the Triumphant." 4.0% ABV, 40 IBU

AWARDS TO KNOW

Among a large host of other reputable awards, Summit Brewing Company has won several medals at the prestigious Great American Beer Festival and World Beer Cup.

1987 Great American Beer Festival: Great Northern Porter, Gold Medal, Porter category

2002 World Beer Cup: Great Northern Porter, Bronze Award, Robust Porter category

2007 Great American Beer Festival: Extra Pale Ale, Bronze Medal, Classic English-Style Pale Ale category

2008 Great American Beer Festival: Extra Pale Ale, Bronze Medal, Classic English-Style Pale Ale category

2010 Great American Beer Festival: Extra Pale Ale, Silver Medal, Classic English-Style Pale Ale category

2010 World Beer Cup: Extra Pale Ale, Gold Award, Classic English-Style Pale Ale category

2012 World Beer Cup: Extra Pale Ale, Silver Award, Classic English-Style Pale Ale category

2014 Great American Beer Festival: Extra Pale Ale, Bronze Medal, Classic English-Style Pale Ale category

2014 World Beer Cup: Extra Pale Ale, Silver Award, Classic English-Style Pale Ale category

2016 Great American Beer Festival: Extra Pale Ale, Gold Medal, Classic English-Style Pale Ale category

2017 Great American Beer Festival: Extra Pale Ale, Silver Medal, Classic English-Style Pale Ale category

2018 Great American Beer Festival: Keller Pils, Gold Medal, Kellerbier/Zwickelbier category

2018 World Beer Cup: Keller Pils, Bronze Award, Kellerbier/Zwickelbier category

The August Schell Brewing Company in New Ulm has been brewing beer in Minnesota for 160 years (minus Prohibition). *Photo courtesy of the August Schell Brewing Company*

AUGUST SCHELL BREWING COMPANY

MINNESOTA'S OLDEST OPERATING BREWERY

New Ulm, Minnesota

Brewery opened: 1860

Barrels produced (2019): 113,900; 2nd largest brewery by production

The Team: Ted Marti, president

Kyle Marti, vice president of operations

Dave Berg, brewmaster

Jeremy Kral, plant manager

Jace Marti, assistant brewmaster

Vance Donner, head brewer

GENERATIONS OF BREWING

Assistant brewmaster Jace Marti represents one of the sixth generation of family ownership at the August Schell Brewing Company. Now in his mid-thirties, he has worked pretty much every job at the brewery, and he has successfully launched several new ventures for the company as well. The innovations and expansions of recent decades have allowed Schell's to continue to grow despite the arrival of dozens and dozens of new breweries on the local scene. At the same time, they are a testament to the qualities that have contributed to Schell's long and fruitful history: expertise, adaptability, and resilience. A brief history of the brewery illustrates the generations of hard work that have allowed Schell's beer to stick around all these years.

The brewery's founder, August Schell, was born in Durbach, Germany, in 1828. He moved to the United States at age twenty, and, unsatisfied with the quality of German beer he was able to find in Minnesota, in 1860 he built his own brewery at thirty-two years old.

"Unfortunately," says the brewery's website, "being a thirsty German doesn't necessarily qualify you to brew beer." So Schell partnered with Jacob Bernhardt, a former brewmaster at the Benzberg Brewery (which became the Minnesota Brewing Company). They produced two hundred barrels of beer in the brewery's first year. Six years later, in 1866, Schell purchased the brewery from Bernhardt.

Over the ensuing decades, the brewery changed ownership from August Schell to his wife, Theresa; then to their sons, Adolph and Otto. After Otto passed away, George Marti, who was married to August Schell's daughter Emma, took over the brewery. Emma later ran the brewery for seven years before handing it off to her son Al. The brewery has remained in the Marti name ever since. The original Schell family crest from Germany, featuring a buck deer, is the crest that Schell's still uses today.

When Prohibition dried up the country in 1919, the Schell Brewing Company fell on tough times. The business made it through by producing near beer, soft drinks, and candy. As the brewery's website

Schell's purchase of Grain Belt Beer in 2002 made it the largest brewery in Minnesota at the time—and gave it the iconic Grain Belt sign overlooking the Mississippi River.

notes: "At the beginning of Prohibition, there were 1,900 breweries. By the end, there were only 600 left, and Schell's was one that weathered the storm. Because the machines had remained in operation through the years, it made the transition back to brewing beer that much easier."

Prohibition was not the last storm Schell's would weather, but the brewery continued to pay homage to its German roots while evolving with a changing American beer industry. The next big shift for Schell's came in 1984, thanks to Ted Marti. After studying at several breweries in Germany, Marti was inspired to have Schell's brew traditional German beers, including a Weizen, which was the first wheat beer brewed in the United States since Prohibition. That recipe is now their seasonal Hefeweizen, and the brewery began exploring more craft beer styles over the next few decades.

To keep up with the growth of the business, Schell's built a new, state-of-the-art brewhouse in 1996 to allow for increased capacity and efficiency. The brewery imported stainless steel kettles from a closed East German brewery, building the connection to brewing traditions from the old country. The company's most significant expansion came in 2002 when it acquired Grain Belt beer—a long-standing Minnesota brand and a longtime competitor of Schell's. It was the largest investment in the company's long history, and the purchase made Schell's the largest brewery in Minnesota at the time.

NEW GENERATION, NEW TRADITIONS

In 2011, Ted Marti's oldest son, Jace, became assistant brewmaster. He had grown up at the brewery and held many jobs within the company.

Jace's earliest memories of the brewery are from when, barely school-age, he poured root beer at one of the brewery's first annual Bock Fests, which began in 1987. Jace laughs as he recalls, "I think I poured like two glasses the whole day because obviously nobody was drinking root beer for the festival." At the time of the gathering's inception, beer festivals were relatively unheard of. At the first Bock Fest, some fifty friends of Ted Marti's showed up to drink beer at the Schell's brewery in New Ulm.

"I was always around the brewery, from my earliest memories," Jace recalls fondly. "I was always at the brewery playing in the gardens. My grandparents lived in the big house, so that's where we would go after school. And we would play in the brewery, climbing on malt stacks and conveyors and all that stuff."

The young Jace was given small jobs like peeling the stickers off mislabeled bottles. He eventually graduated to the bottle house, where he worked the end of the line closing and hand stacking boxes. There was keg washing, wall scraping, kettle cleaning—and all the not-so-glamorous sides of brewery work. His dad assigned him tasks that offered glimpses into different parts of the business, but Jace says his father didn't pressure him into it. "I never thought of doing anything else," Marti says. "I'd grown up into it."

When Marti started studying graphic design in college, it was natural that he apply his talents at the brewery. Through his graphic design work on signage and package design, Marti got to know the sales and distribution side of the brewery business, but, he says, "the ultimate goal was always to get on the brewing side of things."

Marti went off to Germany and Austria to study brewing, and he returned home as assistant brewmaster and with a passion for sour beers. He started the Noble Star Collection at Schell's a year later. This series of Berliner Weisse-style beers are soured in enormous cypress tanks that were originally used for the brewery's non-sour beers dating back to the 1930s. The cypress wood does not hold much flavor, making it a great material in which to ferment lighter beers. Turning these brewing antiques into usable fermenters for the sour program was no small task, however. First, Marti had to find a way to strip the wax layer from inside each tank. After many hours of Googling and plenty of tests on sample boards, he ended up blasting the interior of each massive barrel with dry ice.

In 2015, just two years after Star of the North, the first Noble Star beer, was released, the brewery purchased a piece of land on the north end of New Ulm on which to build a new facility to house this line of beers and serve them to the public in a taproom setting. "Due to the nature of the beer," the brewery notes, "it is ideal for it to age in a separate facility from the remainder of the styles." Opened to the public in 2017, the Starkeller taproom was designed around the cypress fermenters, situating them as a gauntlet honoring beer history. The taproom "affords visitors the opportunity to enjoy a sour from the collection right next to the ten cypress tanks that are aging the future releases."

The new space is a symbolic representation of how Schell's is moving the craft beer industry forward while continuing to brew styles that are true to the brewery's generations-old roots. As Marti told me back in 2017, "These tanks are a footnote in the history of brewing, and to be continuing and starting a new chapter with them in something that they totally weren't intended for is what I love about it. It's part of my family and the brewery's history in a way that is unique only to us. That's why I started this."

While the Starkeller is a beautiful space to celebrate craft beer and the traditional Berliner Weisse style, Marti isn't stopping there. He has plans to open Black Frost Distillery, also in New Ulm, using

The Starkeller taproom is lined with history.

BEER
MINNEAPOLIS.
MINN.

Brewmaster Jace Marti pours samples of one of his Noble Star brews in the Starkeller.

all local Minnesota products. The whiskey-focused distillery will use custom oak barrels made by a Minnesota cooper and corn, rye, and wheat grown in Minnesota, plus barley grown at his business partner's nearby family farm.

As Schell's celebrates 160 years of brewing in Minnesota, it remains an innovative and forward-thinking presence on the craft beer scene locally and nationally.

BEERS TO KNOW

Deer Brand: "A straw-colored classic, our Deer Brand beer is an American lager developed from over a century and a half of continuous brewing history. This pre-Prohibition lager has a mild malt flavor, hop bitterness, and uses our special strain of 'Schell' yeast to make it an Upper Midwest favorite." 4.8% ABV

Hefeweizen: "In 1984, this was the first wheat beer made in the United States after Prohibition, and in 2001 we re-introduced this favorite as an unfiltered Hefeweizen. A slight citric tang and banana aroma make this the perfect beer for working on your lederhosen tan lines." 5.5% ABV, 14 IBU

Light American Lager: "Pale straw in color with a mild maltiness and slight hop aroma, Schell's Light is a perfect option for the drinker who is looking for a robust flavor without all the calories. Weighing in at just 100 calories, the light body and crisp finish will leave you wondering if you are cheating on your diet." 4.0% ABV

Noble Star Collection: "A collection of specialty beers, all Berlin-style wheat beers or Berliner Weisse, aged in rare cypress fermentation tanks Schell's bought in 1936." You can try these on tap in the Starkeller, a taproom and sour aging facility located less than five miles from the Schell's brewery.

Grain Belt Nordeast: An American amber lager featuring light maltiness and hop aroma with a mild bitterness. Smooth taste with excellent drinkability. 4.7% ABV

LIFT BRIDGE BREWING COMPANY

MINNESOTA'S OLDEST OPERATING TAPROOM

Stillwater, Minnesota
Brewery opened: September 2008
Taproom opened: September 2011
Barrels produced (2019): 19,493; 6th largest brewery by production
The Team: Dan Schwarz, cofounder and CEO
Brad Glynn, cofounder and vice president of marketing and taproom operations
Dave Anglum, vice president of sales
Amar Patel, operations and finance manager
Randy Ust, head brewer

BREAKING NEW GROUND

They were just four friends who played poker and homebrewed together on the weekends with their kids in tow. Little did they know, this garage full of buddies and beer would lead to Minnesota's sixth-largest brewery and longest continuously operating taproom.

Brad Glynn, Dan Schwarz, Trevor Cronk, and Jim Pierson are the four owners of Lift Bridge Brewing Company in Stillwater, a historic river town along the St. Croix River. It was during their group homebrewing sessions that the men's entrepreneurial wheels began to turn. *Wouldn't it be great if Stillwater had its own brewery?* As Stillwater residents themselves, they decided they could be the ones to bring craft beer to the community on a commercial level.

Glynn says, "The craft beer movement was in full swing right then. Surly had just opened the year before. We thought, *Okay, there's going to be a lot of changes happening in the beer scene over the next ten years here in the Twin Cities, and we want to be a part of it.*"

Given Stillwater's history of brewing (three breweries operated in the town before Prohibition) and the growing popularity of craft beer in Minnesota in 2008, the team figured opening a locally focused

Lift Bridge cofounder Brad Glynn at the Stillwater brewhouse.

brewery would be a hit. For them, a brewery would blend history, character, friendship, fellowship, celebration, and science.

Unfortunately, only a handful of other non-brewpub breweries were operating in Minnesota at the time, and the path to opening a new brewery was fraught with obstacles. Glynn reflects, "Back then, you had to find your own way a little bit more." Lift Bridge was the only brewery to open in 2008 and only the twelfth overall in Minnesota at the time. In no year since the taproom bill passed in 2011 has only a single brewery opened.

After getting official approval to start their brewery, the four friends bought a warehouse to be the future home of Lift Bridge. In the meantime, they began contract brewing at Flat Earth Brewing in St. Paul, Cold Spring Brewing about twenty miles southwest of St. Cloud, and Stevens Point Brewery in central Wisconsin. In the contract brewing model, the host brewery brews the beer on behalf of another brewery. The beer is legally brewed under the host brewer's license but released under the other brewer's label and brand. Several breweries got their start with contract brewing before opening their own location, including Finnegans Brew Co. (Contract brewing is distinct from an "alternating proprietorship," in which the host brewery leases its equipment and facility to the brand owner, and the beer brewed is legally under the brand owner's brewer's license.)

A year after it started contract brewing, Lift Bridge received its own brewer's license and began operations in its Stillwater brewery facility, allowing the company to brew on its own as well as offer a location to purchase off-sale growlers. The brewery opened with the same fifteen-barrel system that would serve it for over a decade, though the team did significantly expand their fermentation with new tank purchases over that time.

"It was a huge step to move into a building and buy our own equipment," Glynn recalls. "We really didn't want to go broke. We were very cautious because we were friends that came together, we had families, and we certainly didn't want to mortgage our futures."

THE TAPROOM

Because the brewery opened three years before the taproom bill, the Lift Bridge team was not even thinking about holding space for a tasting room or restaurant at their brewery. When the bill passed in May 2011, however, they knew right away how important it was for the brewery to have its own taproom where locals and visitors alike could enjoy the hometown brews. Glynn recollects, "We wanted to really get ahead of that because Stillwater is somewhat of a tourist town, and we had a lot of local friends who really liked our beer, too."

In contrast to the challenges the four friends faced when they first set out to open a brewery in 2008, when Lift Bridge was ready to launch its taproom, it moved through the legal process swiftly. "There is no real reason [to explain] how quickly our [taproom] got approved versus anyone else's, other than expediency of the local government," Glynn says. "Our license is with the City of Stillwater, so it originates there, and they were able to pass [the license] along to the state quicker than some other municipalities that were probably delayed by those specific processes for acquiring the special on-premise license. ... Stillwater has always been supportive of us, and they embraced the new state ruling on taprooms very quickly."

For planning the taproom space, Glynn and team went back to their early visions for their business to draw inspiration. They asked themselves, *What should the taproom space—such an important brand focal point for the brewery—look like?* Glynn says the team took note of regionally focused breweries that hit the sweet spot: Stone Brewing in Escondido, with its sunny southern California beer gardens, and Dogfish Head Brewery, with its "quintessential East Coast beach town" taproom in Rehoboth Beach, Delaware.

Since their backyard beginnings, beer drinking was a social event for the four Lift Bridge owners. They saw beer as a beverage suitable to celebrate everything from weddings to mowing the lawn. Their taproom needed to be a reflection of that sentiment.

A taproom was retrofitted into Lift Bridge's production brewing facility following passage of the taproom bill in 2011.

The owners had to think creatively to get the most out of their given space, as their only option for the taproom was to retrofit the offices in the front of their brewery. The small square footage produced a cozy space with no kitchen and a modest bar.

"We stuck with a lot of natural wood surfaces and communal wood picnic tables that are rough sawn, [which is] reflective of Stillwater's lumber history," says Glynn. The effect is that of a quintessential Minnesota cabin, yet without feeling campy or overdone. The owners hired friendly staff who could lead tours of the brewery and tell its story to visitors and locals, functioning more like park rangers or tour guides than bartenders.

Now, eight years after opening the Lift Bridge taproom, Glynn recognizes that Minnesotans' expectations for what a taproom is and should be have changed. "Back then public perception was just, 'Oh, there's a space we can go buy pints and drink.' It was just cool to go to a brewery and drink there, where you couldn't before in Minnesota." Now, drinkers expect taprooms to have thoughtful design, unique features, and even high-end amenities.

At Lift Bridge, the brewery tour is just as important to the experience as the taproom itself. The tours, once free and now seven dollars with free beer and glassware included, are a hallmark of visiting the brewery. Glynn says they use the tours as a point of education for the consumer: "The craft beer drinker wants to know that they're getting quality beer. If you're paying more for it, that's supposed to be a better experience. Well, why is that? So, on our tours we educate on our ingredients and our process."

That education can happen beyond a guided tour of equipment and ingredients. For Glynn, it happens on the barstool, too. Taproom patrons can try new beers that are still in the research and development stage, earning the ultimate beer hipster claim of trying something before it was cool or popular in cans and on liquor store shelves. That claim is one thing we Minnesotans love about supporting our local taprooms:

A towering maze of barrels and pallets winds through the Lift Bridge storage space.

being there at the beginning of someone's success, supporting them by purchasing pints and sharing reviews with friends, and following the story of the local underdog as they take on Big Beer.

EXPANSION AND GROWTH

By 2020, continued growth and production demands were forcing Lift Bridge out of its original space. The team had been making use of every square inch of their small brewhouse as well as the additional warehouse space across their back parking lot. Both buildings look like production Jenga sets, with barrels, pallets, cans, and ingredients arranged on every stackable surface. A refrigerated semi is parked outside, holding freshly filled cans ready to be taken away by a distributor. Contract brewers help Lift Bridge keep up with production, but those logistics can be complicated.

The brewery that Lift Bridge was when it opened in 2008 clearly no longer exists. It has gone far beyond a group of homebrewing friends selling growlers out of a warehouse. The delivery methodology has expanded from Glynn driving beer around in his truck to relationships with several distribution partners. In 2018, Lift Bridge produced 14,425 barrels, making it the ninth-largest brewery by production volume in Minnesota that year. It produced an additional 5,000 barrels through contract brewing at Summit Brewing, Brew Detroit, MKE Brewing, and Cold Spring Brewing. No amount of trunk space can deliver that much beer.

In addition, in January 2019, Lift Bridge launched a line of hard seltzers, swooping in on an emerging market that was dominated by wine coolers, Mike's Hard Lemonade, and White Claw Hard Seltzers. In a February 2019 *City Pages* article by Jerard Fagerberg about the fast-growing hard-seltzer market, Glynn said he began noticing that his brewers were bringing White Claw to company parties, and it led him to think about how Lift Bridge might enter that market. "I know there are big corporations doing them," he said in *City Pages*, "but how would it look if there was a craft brewery doing it here? There's certainly a market for it. Of course, we don't have the marketing dollars of the bigger brands, but we can start here, locally, and tell our story like we did with beer." All of Lift Bridge's canned and on-tap hard seltzers are five percent ABV, and they come in such varieties as Northwoods Juice Box (sweet apple and tart cranberry flavors), Citrus Blend (grapefruit, lemon, lime, and orange flavors), and Blue Agave Margarita (lime, orange, and tequila flavors).

With one eye fixed on steady, reliable growth and the other looking to the future of the industry, Lift Bridge is not showing any signs of dropping in the production volume ranks for its beers. Hindered only by a small brewhouse overflowing with pallets of product, what they needed in order to keep growing was more space. At the time of this writing, Lift Bridge is planning to break ground on a massive new Stillwater taproom and brewery space. Just like before, they are taking it slow and investing wisely. "We don't want to go broke building a Taj Mahal–style brewery," says Glynn.

"Our primary driver for this expansion is the production," he continues. "We really are a production brewery first and foremost." Distributed beer—kegs at bars and restaurants, cans at liquor stores—is the largest profit center and the focus of the business. Lift Bridge's owners don't want their profits to rely too heavily on folks showing up to the taproom—they worry that it's putting all their eggs in one basket, especially for a brewery that built its business on distribution prior to the taproom bill.

The new brewery is a proposed $10 million, 35,000-square-foot facility that will dwarf Lift Bridge's original space. It will allow the brewery not only to expand its operations but also to streamline it. That means no more storage trailers in the parking lot and fewer barrel mazes to go through to find the quality control lab.

"This new brewery will accommodate our growth up to about 70,000 barrels, which we expect in a 10-year plan," Glynn told Mary Divine of the *Pioneer Press*. "We still want to grow steady—at about a 30 percent growth rate, which we have done for the past five years."

They hope to open the new taproom in 2021.

BEERS TO KNOW

Farm Girl Saison: "Perfectly balanced and moderately sweet with light citrus notes and a distinct spiciness from choice Belgian yeasts. Farm Girl Saison was lovingly created for the wife of a cofounder, inspired by the farm she grew up on." Lift Bridge's flagship beer is still their best seller. 5.5% ABV, 12 IBU

Hop Dish IPA: "Aggressively hopped IPA with aromas of citrus, fruit, pine. A subtle malt sweetness with notes of caramel." 6.5% ABV, 75 IBU

Juice-Z NE IPA: This New England–style IPA, "a monstrous blend of fruit-forward hops[,] is balanced out with golden malt, wheat, and oats." 5% ABV, 40 IBU

Mango Blonde: "This beer is a limited release experience of summer coming. The aroma of a tropical breeze from a fresh mango grove leads into a light-bodied blonde ale, finishing with a subtle mango sweetness that does not overpower the golden malt." 4.75% ABV, 15 IBU

Silhouette: "Brewed in the style of an imperial stout. Aromas of coffee, molasses, chocolate, and prune meld with an intense dark roasted character. This beer is complex, rich, and full bodied." 11% ABV, 50 IBU

AWARDS TO KNOW

In addition to earning "best beer" honors in several categories, Lift Bridge has won recognition for its bartenders and its beer names in *The Growler* magazine's "Kind-of-a-Big-Deal" annual readers' choice awards. The Tastings awards are bestowed by the Beverage Testing Institute.

2016 *The Growler* "Kind-of-a-Big-Deal": Farm Girl Saison, Best Belgian Style

2017 *The Growler* "Kind-of-a-Big-Deal": Farm Girl Saison, Best Belgian Style

2017 Tastings award: Silhouette, Gold Medal

2018 *The Growler* "Kind-of-a-Big-Deal": Farm Girl Saison, Best Belgian Style

2018 *The Growler* "Kind-of-a-Big-Deal": Mango Blonde, Best Fruit Beer

2018 *The Growler* "Kind-of-a-Big-Deal": Mango Blonde, Best Session Beer

2019 Tastings award: 93x Brotherhood American Lager, Silver Medal

2019 Tastings award: Farm Girl Saison, Gold Medal

2019 Tastings award: Fireside Flannel Brown Ale, Silver Medal

2019 Tastings award: Juice-Z NE IPA, Gold Medal

A Lift Bridge flight illustrates the range of beers—and hard seltzer—produced by the groundbreaking brewery.

BENT PADDLE BREWING COMPANY

A STAPLE IN THE LAKE SUPERIOR PORT TOWN OF DULUTH

Duluth, Minnesota
Opened: May 2013
Barrels produced (2019): 14,474; 9th largest in state by production
The Team: Colin Mullen, cofounder, president, and director of brewery communications
Laura Mullen, cofounder and vice president of outreach and events
Bryon Tonnis, cofounder, CEO, and director of brewing operations
Karen Tonnis, cofounder and vice president of operations

THE ORIGIN STORY

Laura Mullen entered the craft beer industry in 2004–05, when there were only twenty-some breweries in the state. Little did she know how large of a role she would play in developing our state's craft beer culture. At the time, she was running an events company, and she was tasked with planning Arbor Fest, a beer festival for the Family Tree Clinic in St. Paul. The clinic had worked exclusively with distributors in the past and featured regional breweries rather than focusing on local ones. Mullen thought a local clinic should feature local talent. She started her cold calls for the event by looking for someone to give a homebrewing demonstration, which would also serve as practice for her cold calls to breweries that had never heard of her little festival.

Mullen started by Googling homebrew supply stores. Midwest Supplies came up first in the search results. Laura recalls, "So I called Midwest. I said, 'Can I please speak to someone in marketing?' And they laughed at me and they connected me on the phone to someone named Colin, and we had this really awesome phone call. Long story short, we're married now." Long before those nuptials, however, Colin agreed to do the demonstration, and Laura's small fundraising festival was a success.

A couple months before her own festival, Mullen learned of a beer festival called Autumn Brew Review. The Minnesota Craft Brewers Guild

The four founders of Bent Paddle Brewing Company enjoy the fruits of their labor in their Duluth taproom. *Photo by JaneCane Photography*

has hosted the festival since 2001, starting with a small collection of breweries. Many of the brewers Mullen had cold-called for her own festival would be in attendance, so she decided to buy a ticket and meet them all in person. This was also where she met Colin in person for the first time.

The following year, the guild was not able to bring the festival back to its location at Peavey Plaza in Minneapolis. In addition, ticket sales were suffering and the volunteers running the festival were disengaged. The guild considered canceling the fest altogether. Colin, who was a member of the Craft Brewers Guild, recommended the guild reach out to Laura's professional events company. The guild eventually hired her to run and revive the festival, and gosh did she make that happen. She relocated Autumn Brew Review to the Grain Belt Brewery Complex in Northeast Minneapolis and opened presale tickets online. If it rained on the day of the festival, folks who had bought their tickets ahead of time would likely still show up, so the guild wouldn't lose their shirts by depending on only same-day ticket sales at the door. Supported by Laura's promotions and organizational skills, the festival sold out for the first time: "So then the next like three or four years, that [festival] sold out within thirty seconds to two minutes."

With Laura's event planning company taking off, Colin stepped in to help her with festival setup, organizational duties, graphic design, and other on-site work. He was still working part-time at Midwest Supplies and part-time at Barley John's Brewpub in New Brighton. Meantime, between planning and promoting two major festivals and doing administrative work, the guild accounted for 50 percent of Laura's business. She recalls, "My phone number became the guild's office."

TAPPING INTO DULUTH

Laura and Colin married in September 2008, just nine days apart from their future business partners, Karen and Bryon Tonnis. The Tonnises met in college at the University of Minnesota Duluth. After leaving college, Bryon got a job brewing at Twin Ports (now Thirsty Pagan) in Superior, Wisconsin, just across the St. Louis River from Duluth. In 2004, he earned his International Diploma in Brewing Technology from the Siebel Institute of Technology and World Brewing Academy, a combination program out of Chicago and Munich. He assumed the head brewer role at Rock Bottom in Minneapolis after Todd Haug left to go to Surly Brewing.

The Tonnises and Mullens met at craft beer festivals and other industry events. They were similar in age, shared a love of Duluth (Laura's hometown), and enjoyed paddling Minnesota and Wisconsin waters. The partnership was inevitable.

At a 2010 Movember fundraiser at the Blue Nile restaurant in Minneapolis, Laura sat with the Tonnises, watching Colin's band play. At the time, Laura was looking to leave her events company; although the business was successful, she was starting to burn out. Colin encouraged her to broaden her business model, to which she responded, "We need to focus on craft beer and I want to move to Duluth and we need to have kids and we need to get this train going."

At the Blue Nile event, Laura asked Karen, "What are your future plans?" Karen responded, "I don't know. What are your future plans?" Self-reportedly a little drunk, Laura insisted, "The boys should talk!"

The "boys" enjoyed a few hours of beer and conversation together. It came out that both couples had the same dream: to open a brewery in Duluth. Laura knew from experience that running a company alone or within a single family unit was exhausting. If a family emergency came up, she had to decide if her client or her family would come first. Joining forces with colleagues would allow them to better distribute responsibilities, both professional and personal.

During this postrecession period, Laura was receiving calls at the guild from laid-off money managers and longtime homebrewers who were looking to open their own breweries. Noticing this trend as well as the buzz growing in the Twin Cities around craft beer, she knew their team had to make their move quickly in Duluth, a market that already had several brewpubs and small breweries at that point but was relatively untouched by large-scale breweries.

The couples spent 2011 writing their business plan, with all four as equal partners. They scoped out a location that had good visibility from the highway that runs through Duluth, was relatively inexpensive for the 10,600 square feet of space, and had thick concrete slabs able to support the brewing equipment. Laura remembers, "We were ready to go, and then the Surly Bill happens. So we were like, *We better make room for a taproom!* We carved out 1,200 square feet." Thus, the Bent Paddle brewery and taproom were both born.

Two and half years after that fateful conversation at the Blue Nile, the Mullens and Tonnises opened their Duluth brewery and taproom to great success. "It went really, really, really well," says Laura. "We started with twelve accounts in Duluth, self-distributing. We only had us and one sales guy and a couple of taproom beertenders, and that's it. We were doing everything: answering every phone call, doing our own books and all the marketing, packaging our own beer, delivering our own beer." The foursome accomplished all this work at the brewery while both couples were raising newborns, who were born three days apart.

The team hit their two-year sales goals in six months and their seven-year business plan by year two. By the time they signed with a beer distributor, they had a two-hundred-account waiting list.

Laura says, "We had this philosophy about it: the blue-sky theory of *get ahead of everything*, because you could really feel the bubble coming. All these breweries were starting to open in the Twin Cities, where you hadn't seen a new distribution brewery open for years, and now it was happening." The goal, Laura adds, was "to own Duluth. I always say, 'I want our beer at every fish bar just like Summit is.' You can go to a bar in Aurora and there's [Summit] EPA on tap or in a can. I want Bent Paddle to have that hold in Minnesota. We thought a way of doing that is to get everywhere before all this competition. And it worked." Indeed

Bent Paddle's beer became so popular so fast, the increased production demands forced the company to expand to a larger brewing facility within just a few years of opening.

it did: by 2019, Bent Paddle was distributing to 2,700 accounts, covering all of Minnesota, all of North Dakota, and about half of Wisconsin.

EXPANSION

One day in the spring of 2015, Laura and Karen walked to the building next door to their brewery, which was about to be vacated by the current occupant. The taproom and office spaces at Bent Paddle's original brewery were getting cramped, and the two women saw opportunity in the neighboring brick-and-timber building, which had a second-floor space built out with attractive cubicles. "That's when we started thinking about building a new taproom," says Laura.

Because Minnesota state law requires that any beer poured at a taproom has to be brewed in a facility immediately adjacent to the taproom, the Bent Paddle team built a $300,000 "mini-brewery" in the new building to produce the taproom's beer, while all production for distribution continued at the original location.

The new taproom, which opened in April 2018, is a gorgeous destination space with thoughtful design features. Tilework along the bar evokes visions of barley and water, and local art such as images of the aurora borealis and a painted Sanborn canoe paddle—along with several other paddles, appropriately—adorn the brick walls. *The* bent paddle that is the brewery's namesake, a mash mixer that broke during Bryon's last brew at Rock Bottom Brewery, hangs between two enormous windows. At 5,500 square feet, the million-plus-dollar expansion elevated Bent Paddle from a distribution brewery to a destination brewery and taproom that embodies everything folks love about the city on the shores of Lake Superior. It is luxurious in craftsmanship and as inviting as a lakeshore cabin.

"It has been amazing," says Laura of the new space. "It's like a test kitchen for us, which is awesome." Visitors to the brewery get to test out the fifteen-barrel pilot batches of new and exciting recipes. Mullen says their taproom brewer, Neil Caron from Thirsty Pagan, "has a background of lots of beer styles and being inventive, and it's a really fun playground for him."

The Bent Paddle taproom offers a visual treat as well as a gustatory one.

Bent Paddle's new taproom is part of a larger revitalization of the Lincoln Park neighborhood of Duluth. Like the Mullens and the Tonnises did, other folks are relocating to Duluth, whether it's because they grew up in the city and are returning to raise a family, attended college there and fell in love with the place, or have always dreamt about moving north. "There's so much entrepreneurial energy here right now," says Mullen.

With the growth of the neighborhood, several new restaurants have also opened. The Bent Paddle crew has no intention of being in direct competition with those establishments. Instead, they've teamed up with local vendors to coordinate food delivery to the taproom. "Yes, the customers in this room are clients," Laura explains, "but more so the bars, liquor stores, and restaurants that buy 95 percent of our beer are our core customers."

WHAT'S UP WITH DULUTH?

Bent Paddle's brand is intimately tied up in the city of Duluth. Describe the brewery's ideal customer, and you couldn't throw a rock in Duluth without hitting someone who fits it. As Laura describes it: "They drive a Subaru that has some sort of a roof rack, and there's a dog involved, and they're wearing Birkenstocks. It's a Duluth-style thing, and that's what we wanted our brand to be." And that brand attracts a regular cast of returning customers. On a Saturday afternoon in the taproom, Mullen could spot as many as twenty people who visit on a weekly basis.

Minnesotans have a fascination with the Great Lakes port city of Duluth. For some, the draw is the city's parks and trails. "It's just a beautiful port town that opens to the north woods," Mullen explains. Duluth itself is home to 6,834 acres of city parkland, 178 miles of wooded trails, and 16 designated trout streams. It's also a natural stop for people on the way to destinations further along the shore, such as Gooseberry Falls State Park, the Gunflint Trail, and the Boundary Waters Canoe Area. Perhaps it's no surprise that *Outside* magazine called Duluth the "best town ever" in 2014.

For other Duluth lovers, it's the lake that calls them. The expansive waters of Lake Superior are both a source of economic development and a powerful, almost mystical force in Duluth culture. The lake especially calls to brewers for the quality of its water. As the Bent Paddle website explains, "The City of Duluth was selected by our team primarily because of the great brewing water. ... Lake Superior is 10% of the world's fresh water and 100% of our beer is made with that water. It is incredibly soft and mimics the water of Pilsen, Czech Republic, the birthplace of Pilseners." In addition to Bent Paddle, Duluth is home to a handful of other fantastic breweries, the iconic Fitger's brewpub, and a couple other small brewpubs; Castle Danger Brewing is fewer than thirty miles up the shore in Two Harbors.

Most people who love Duluth's natural beauty and Lake Superior's majestic shores feel personally compelled to protect them. Bent Paddle also took that cause to heart, launching several sustainability programs to preserve its hometown. The brewery works with local vendors to produce recycled plastic tap handles and tablecloths, and restaurants that deliver to the taproom are required to use bio-compostable containers and utensils or offer reusable alternatives. The brewhouse is set up for energy efficiency, and the team originally purchased a biodiesel delivery van to run energy-efficient routes. Bent Paddle also works with a local organization that employs people with disabilities to collect their stretch wrap and other stretchable plastic for recycling.

Even the taproom décor reuses old materials that would have otherwise gone to waste: the entryway chandelier is built out of old plastic four-pack and six-pack carriers, and the taproom chandeliers are rusted-out firepits from Duluth's Bentleyville Christmas light display. "They brought them over for free because it's Duluth," says Mullen with a laugh.

Bent Paddle's valiant fight to protect its city can come at a cost, however. Bent Paddle and several other local businesses spoke out against the proposed location of a new copper-nickel mine, objecting to its potential for polluting Lake Superior. In retaliation, according to the *Star Tribune*, the Silver Bay City Council voted to stop selling Bent Paddle beer at its municipal liquor store. Privately owned liquor stores in the area also decided to boycott the brewery.

Though it may have ruffled some feathers, Bent Paddle Brewing remains a leader in craft brewing and an anchor in one of Minnesota's favorite towns—the gateway to the north.

BEERS TO KNOW

Bent Hop: "An unexpected visual bend to an American India Pale Ale, this style is one that stands out in a crowd, or if you're more like us—[is] enjoyed at a campsite ... with no crowd. This nontraditional IPA is golden in color with an enormous floral/citrus hop aroma and a supporting malt profile." This year-round golden IPA accounts for about 40 percent of Bent Paddle's total beer sales. 6.2% ABV, 68 IBU

Classic: "Bent Paddle Classic is an easygoing beer for any beer drinker. Straightforward and light with a smooth, creamy finish. This beer brings things back to the basics. Sometimes, all you want is a beer that tastes like beer. Classic." 5.0% ABV, 18 IBU

14° ESB: "Our well-rounded approach to the classic British Ale. There's middle of the road, and there's middle of the river. And if there's one thing that's important in the middle of the river—it's balance. Our ESB is incredibly well balanced with a slight toasted malt flavor, traditional British hop accents with just a hint of pine and citrus from the unexpected Amarillo/Ahtanum dry-hop." This Extra Special Bitter amber ale has won three medals at the highly respected Great American Beer Festival. 5.6% ABV, 32 IBU

Black Ale: "Brewed to be a smooth, chocolatey, semi-roasted ale that bridges the islands of porter and stout. ... This Black Ale drinks like a porter but is opaque like a stout. Brewed with a generous amount of oats to round out the flavor."

Cold Press Black: "Our Black Ale infused with cold-press coffee, Cold Press Black is a beer that started around relationships and community. Our partnership with our local roaster, Duluth Coffee Company, expanded in 2018 to include the coffee farmer as well!" This Minnesota favorite tops many coffee beer lists. 6% ABV, 35 IBU

Double Shot Double Black: An annual release that has racked up its share of awards and sells out quickly. "This robust version of our Black Ale features a smooth, chocolatey, semi-roasted malt profile that sweetly balances out the doubled strength. Notes of oak and whiskey from an extended aging period in bourbon barrels create a welcoming warmth."

Kanu Session Pale Ale: "The 'Weekend Warrior,' the 'Tin Tank,' the 'Camp Classic'—most canoeists experienced their first paddle in an aluminum canoe. It's perfect for the beginner: rugged and stable, not to mention glaringly bright! Kanu Session Pale Ale pays homage to that nostalgic entry point into paddling life. Brilliant hop expression with a structural malt 'hull,' this session pale is designed to accompany your journey. Grab a 12'er and climb aboard our craft!" 4.8% AVB, 48 IBU

Trampled: Bent Paddle brewed this collaboration beer with Trampled by Turtles, a Duluth-founded and internationally known bluegrass band. The brewery's description of the beer is heavily infused with the band's song titles: "Calling all Wild Animals & Winners. This Hometown Collaboration takes us Right Back Where We Started and is a spotlight on the creativity that emanates from our beloved city on the hill. Nothing pairs better with listening to music than a beer in your hand—especially a beer that harmonizes in tune with the band. Trampled American Golden Ale plays forth with a soft malt flavor and a resonant hop tone, creating a balanced volume of flavor. This beer might have you Drinkin' In the Mornin,' but don't worry, you won't have to Wait So Long to enjoy another one!" 4.6% ABV, 20 IBU

Venture Pils: "This craft lager harmonizes noble hops and premium malts found in North America and Europe. Brewed with pristine Lake Superior water, this straw-colored pilsener takes on characteristics of Bohemia and northern Germany with a touch of American inventiveness. Refreshingly crisp with a gentle floral hop aroma." 5.0% ABV, 38 IBU

Beer flights in the taproom are an opportunity to sample this Duluth brewery's impressive beer list.

AWARDS TO KNOW

Bent Paddle has earned a host of accolades, from beer festival awards to recognition as a leading local business and for community service. The brewery has also won numerous awards recognizing it as one of the best breweries and taprooms in Minnesota.

2014 Autumn Brew Review: Double Shot Double Black, Best Beer

2014 Great American Beer Festival: 14° ESB, Bronze Medal, Extra Special Bitter category

2014 *The Growler* "Kind-of-a-Big-Deal" Award: Black Ale, Best Porter

2014 *The Growler* "Kind-of-a-Big-Deal" Award: Venture Pils, Best Local and Overall Lager/Pilsner

2015 Great American Beer Festival: 14° ESB, Silver Medal, Extra Special Bitter category

2016 *The Growler* "Kind-of-a-Big-Deal" Award: Venture Pils, Best Pilsner

2017 Great American Beer Festival: 14° ESB, Gold Medal, Extra Special Bitter category

2018 Great American Beer Festival: Saison, Gold Medal, Classic Saison category

2019 Brewers Cup Awards: Double Shot Double Black, First Place, Non-Sour Barrel-Aged Beers

2019 Brewers Cup Awards: 14° ESB, Third Place, Amber/Red Ales

INDEED BREWING COMPANY

NORTHEAST MINNEAPOLIS'S ORIGINAL TAPROOM

Minneapolis, Minnesota
Opened: August 2012
Barrels produced (2019): 15,836; 8th largest in state by production
The Team: Nathan Berndt, cofounder and president
Tom Whisenand, cofounder and CEO

HUMBLE BEGINNINGS

Tom Whisenand's passion for beer began like it has for so many other brewery owners: drinking and homebrewing craft beer. Determined to find his place in the industry, he got his start in the business washing growlers and eventually went on to become the owner of one of the most successful and respected craft breweries in the state.

Whisenand's first real introduction to all that craft beer had to offer was while he worked as a photojournalism intern on the East Coast in the early 2000s. Compared to Minnesota, which had just a couple of large distribution breweries, it was a haven—and an inspiration, in particular the beers coming out of New Hampshire, Vermont, and Maine. His newfound excitement about craft beer soon prompted Whisenand to explore homebrewing.

After his job as a staff photojournalist with the *Star Tribune* dried up with the financial collapse of 2008, Whisenand pivoted and took a position waiting tables at Town Hall. Town Hall, a Minneapolis brewpub that now has multiple restaurant locations, is an icon in Minnesota beer. More than a handful of local brewers and industry professionals cut their teeth there since it opened in 1997. And Town Hall is where Whisenand really dug into craft beer. While homebrewing on the side, he crossed the line from the front of the house to working in the brewhouse at Town Hall. He would fill growlers in the mornings, nap on the grain sacks in the malt room after his brewhouse work, and then earn his rent money waiting tables in the restaurant each night.

Tom Whisenand of Indeed Brewing helped lead the way in turning Northeast Minneapolis into a taproom haven.

During his time at Town Hall, Whisenand got to know the owner, the head brewer, and other folks in the industry. He recalls fondly how his career shift was largely driven by the personalities and people around him. When he worked in newspapers, Whisenand felt that people weren't necessarily thinking outside the box. "We were selling something that nobody wanted to buy," he says, "but [beer] was this different world where people were relaxed, fun, and not stuffy. We were selling something everybody wanted to buy." As it turns out, beer is always in demand. Whisenand says, "That really stuck with me and is what eventually led me to where we are today."

Whisenand decided he wanted to start his own business, and beer was what he wanted to do. But he didn't decide to start a brewery just because his friends or uncles enjoyed his homebrews. He understood that "brewing is only one small part of running a brewery." His goal, surely, was to make and sell great beer. But Whisenand had seen too many other breweries hit the mark in one area of their business and miss it altogether in another. His approach was to strive to do a great job at everything.

To run a commercial brewery with no commercial brewing experience or an event space without having ever planned events is no easy feat. But, as Whisenand recalls, he and his business partner, Nathan Berndt, planned on "hiring people smarter than us and better than us to make it happen." Just over seven years after the brewery opened, Indeed now employs more than five dozen people and has become a fixture in a corner of Northeast Minneapolis; Indeed was even named a top place to work by the *Star Tribune* in 2017.

OPENING NORTHEAST'S ORIGINAL TAPROOM

When Indeed Brewing opened its brewery and taproom in August 2012, just fifteen months had passed since the taproom bill was signed into law, and only a few taprooms were operating in Minnesota. There was Lift Bridge in Stillwater, Fulton in the North Loop of Minneapolis, and Harriet in south Minneapolis. Fulton and Lift Bridge were brewing and had established their brands before opening a taproom, and Harriet opened as a result of Minneapolis's passage of the growler bill in 2010. Indeed would be one of the first of its kind: it would open a taproom at the same time as it opened a brewery. Plus, it was the first in a neighborhood that would become a hub for craft breweries in the next several years.

Originally, Indeed was planned as a production-only brewery. While Whisenand was developing the business plan, however, the taproom bill passed and changed the game entirely. "If the taproom law hadn't changed and we had proceeded with our [original] business plan," he says, "I don't think we'd be sitting here right now." And right now Indeed is sitting as the eighth-largest brewery in the state.

Operating a production brewery without a taproom would have been a heavy weight to carry. Whisenand says managing production, packaging, and wholesale is "really hard until you're a certain size." Wholesale distribution requires an economy of scale, and it's a tough road to get there. Having a taproom, Whisenand points out, gives you additional options for building the business. "The taproom has been a huge part of the energy and, honestly, the financials of this business,"

Northeast Minneapolis's original taproom is located in the historic Solar Arts Building. Built in 1914 as a tire factory, the hundred-plus-year-old building is home to many artist studios today.

he says. "It's afforded us the ability to do a lot of things that we wouldn't have been able to do without it. It made this business viable, especially because we wanted to be in the city."

Indeed is managing its production with self-distribution, which is legal for breweries that produce fewer than 25,000 barrels of beer in a year. Whisenand says that self-distributing, rather than partnering with a wholesaler, is "great for our brand. Through all the growth in the industry and the number of brands out there, we've been able to have our sales people and our drivers talk only about Indeed. It's been a hugely beneficial part of our business."

Even with the successful self-distribution operation out of its Minneapolis brewery, Indeed has something bigger in mind. Whisenand says, "Ultimately we've always modeled ourselves as being a wholesale, production brewery with a great taproom." Whisenand wants to carry Indeed's energy and reputation toward doubling the brewery's production volume and selling beer to every state that borders Minnesota. That goal is difficult to accomplish on one's own, and Indeed will soon hit the 25,000-barrel self-distribution cap, so the brewery will have to take on distribution partners. But first, they took on a new taproom.

MILWAUKEE BOUND

Whisenand and Indeed had decided they wanted to open a second taproom to expand the business, but because Minnesota law allows only one taproom in the state per brewery, Indeed looked east, to the neighboring state of Wisconsin. In November 2018, a little more than six years after opening its brewery in Northeast Minneapolis, Indeed Brewing announced plans to expand to Milwaukee, the town also known as Brew City.

When Indeed launched its Minneapolis taproom in 2013, it had been a plan B, a pivot from the original plans to operate as a production brewery, to take advantage of a new opportunity after the taproom bill passed. The changes left the partners strapped for cash, however, and unable to afford an architect or a designer to help them develop the taproom space. So Whisenand called on his friend Bob, a woodworker

Hoping to replicate the feel of the Minneapolis taproom in its new Milwaukee location, the Indeed team went on a vast search to find chairs to match those in the original taproom.

from northern Wisconsin. The two of them sketched out the location on a napkin, and Bob took it from there. He procured lumber for the wainscoting and banquette seating to create a homey atmosphere in the industrial Northeast neighborhood.

For the Milwaukee expansion, the Indeed team modeled the new taproom after Bob's work in Minneapolis. The team in Milwaukee even went so far as to include the same chairs as those in the Minneapolis taproom. In Minneapolis, the chairs came for free from the clubroom in an old publishing company. In Milwaukee, finding the chairs was a different story. First, they found the chair supplier. But the supplier didn't make those chairs any more. Then, they found a guy in the Indiana town where the chairs were made. He doesn't make the chairs, but he does collect and sell them. It was an adventure—and an expensive one at $350 a chair—but they carried one of the symbols of the Minneapolis taproom over the border and through the very dense woods to Brew City.

As Indeed grows from its role as the first taproom in Minnesota's greatest craft beer neighborhood to operating a second location in Milwaukee, it remains a neighborhood fixture. Even as the state's

Featuring exposed brick walls and rich wood furnishings, the atmosphere in the Indeed taproom is more like that of a comfortable pub than an old industrial warehouse.

eighth-largest brewery, Indeed still hosts community fundraisers, features local artists, and serves pints at its cozy taproom bar.

BEERS TO KNOW

Indeed has churned out dozens of fantastic beers over the years. The beers' labels, designed in collaboration with local artist Chuck U, are visual treats on Minnesota liquor store shelves.

Day Tripper Pale Ale: "Four pounds of hops per barrel give this West Coast–style pale ale a heady, dank, and citrus-laced aroma supported by a complex and subtly sweet malt backbone." 5.4% ABV, 45 IBU

Flavorwave IPA: "Bright golden and lit with a gentle haze, Flavorwave IPA delivers with pineapple, citrus, and stone fruit aromas and a rush of fruity, tropical hop flavor." 6.2% ABV, 73 IBU

Mexican Honey Imperial Lager: "Humming with a citrus and floral fiesta for the senses, Mexican Honey Imperial Lager is brewed with Mexican orange blossom honey and Amarillo hops. Refreshing and dangerously smooth, this award-winning cerveza is all buzz, no bite." 8% ABV, 17 IBU

Wooden Soul: A series of sour, funky, wild, and barrel-aged beers. These beers aren't among the brewery's top sellers, but they are an important part of Indeed's range of styles, with a small but devoted following.

AWARDS TO KNOW

In addition to its beer awards, Indeed has also been recognized for the label art by local artist Chuck U.

2014 Great American Beer Festival: Mexican Honey Imperial Lager, Silver Medal, Specialty Honey Beer category

2016 Brussels Beer Challenge: Day Tripper Pale Ale, Bronze Medal, Pale & Amber Ale: American Pale Ale category

2016 Brussels Beer Challenge: LSD Honey Ale, Silver Medal, Flavoured Beer: Herb & Spice category

Indeed Brewing offers a large selection of regular and rotating options from behind the taproom bar.

2017 European Beer Star Awards: Mexican Honey Imperial Lager, Bronze Medal, Specialty Honey Beer category

2018 European Beer Star Awards: B-Side Pils, Bronze Medal, Keller Pils category

2019 Brussels Beer Challenge: Mexican Honey Imperial Lager, Bronze Medal, Flavoured Beer: Honey Beer category

2019 Copa Cervezas de América: Flavorwave, Gold Medal, American IPA category

2019 Copa Cervezas de América: Strawberry Fields, Gold Medal, Wild Specialty Beer category

2019 European Beer Star Awards: LSD Honey Ale, Gold Medal, Herb & Spice Beer category

Approaching the HammerHeart taproom feels like stumbling upon something out of Narnia.

HAMMERHEART BREWING COMPANY

HONORING THE OLD NORDIC AND CELTIC CULTURES

Lino Lakes, Minnesota
Opened: August 2013
Barrels produced (2019): 507; 91st largest in state by production
The Team: Nathaniel Chapman, owner
Austin Lunn, head brewer

BLACK METAL BREWER

Much of my time at the HammerHeart taproom with head brewer Austin Lunn was off the record while I enjoyed a wide sampling of smoked beers, which frankly knocked me on my ass. He told tales of *Gjærskrik* or "gjærkauk," the old Norwegian farmhouse tradition in which the brewer screams at the yeast while pitching it (a step in the brewing process), and he poured me samples of the first smoked beer he ever tried—an urbock from Schlenkerla Brewery. We discussed politics as well as the chemistry of Kveik, a recently popularized Norwegian yeast strain. Drinking at HammerHeart was more than just another taproom visit. It was an immersive cultural drinking experience.

And the fact is, there is no other brewery like HammerHeart in Minnesota—and probably not for many, many miles beyond it as well. The small facility looks like a cabin in the woods, and it feels as cozy as one.

To get to HammerHeart's taproom, you pass through a small grove of pines before reaching a large front door that is adorned with Norse imagery hand carved by Lunn. Inside, the taproom is paneled in pine and has a low ceiling supported by exposed wood beams. Warm lights enclosed in mason jars illuminate the many antlers decorating the walls, and an array of handmade tap handles beckons you to the half-dozen seat bar.

With lots of natural-wood features and antler details, the HammerHeart taproom has the feel of a north woods cabin.

The beer list offers things like peat-smoked Irish red ales and imperial pumpkin stouts with chipotle peppers. HammerHeart specializes in smoked and barrel-aged beers, and Lunn does not shy away from that very particular niche.

Lunn explains that he and his brother-in-law, Nathaniel Chapman, could have opened their little smoked-beer brewery in Minneapolis, where more of their specialty market might be found, but they would have lost something in the process. The aesthetic of the brewery, from the outside in, was designed to look like Meduseld, an ornate hall amongst the mountains in *Lord of the Rings*. (Fittingly, the name *Meduseld* means “mead-hall.”) The space lends itself to the relatively sleepy town of Lino Lakes just north of the Twin Cities better than it would to Minneapolis’s urban cityscape.

HammerHeart’s beer and taproom go hand in hand (or Haand, if you will). Both the beer and the space are inspired by Lunn’s time working as an apprentice at Haandbryggeriet brewery in Norway. Plus, the Norse imagery and interest in Norse culture also connects with Lunn’s participation in the black metal music scene. In 2002, Lunn dropped out of college to play in a metal band.

Lunn, who grew up in Tennessee and lived in Kentucky for a decade, is covered in tattoos and wears mostly black clothing with heavy metal imagery, so a friendly Minnesota gal like myself might assume he has a gruff personality to match his harsh exterior. In reality, Lunn’s personality and politics are informed by empathy and equity, which is common in the black metal scene. This attitude is present in the HammerHeart taproom, too, where people are readily ejected for intolerance, including a range of behaviors such as using homophobic slurs, being sexist, or on one occasion even going so far as to espouse neo-Nazi views.

An interest in Norse culture is also common in the black metal scene, and Lunn is no exception. He’s well educated in Norse history, language, and beer. Lunn and his wife, Bekah, whom he met while touring with his band, married in the style of a traditional Viking wedding, which took six months of research to plan. After their wedding, the couple was traveling in Norway when they came across

Head brewer Austin Lunn enjoys one of his beers at the bar at HammerHeart.

a brewery in the town of Drammen: Haandbryggeriet. When Lunn expressed interest, the folks at the brewery offered the homebrewer an apprenticeship. Lunn politely declined and returned stateside with Bekah.

Back at home, Lunn played in his band and started a career working with at-risk youth by day. However, after seven years at that job, Lunn says, "my empathy gland was wearing out."

So, when Bekah's brother called him about starting a craft brewery, Lunn considered it seriously. He knew he didn't have the commercial experience to back up his homebrewing skills, so he wasn't on board with the idea immediately, but he did have that offer for an apprenticeship from that brewery in Norway. He reached out to the folks at Haand to ask if the offer was still on the table. They told him to pack his bags, and he headed back to Norway.

Lunn spent three months in Norway on a tourist visa as an apprentice at Haand. Because he was only able to stay in Norway for that short span to complete what was usually a six-month apprenticeship, it was a jam-packed experience. Lunn returned home with not only commercial brewing experience but also the ability to make beer he loved that was steeped in a history he appreciated. Lunn and Chapman were finally ready to open their own brewery.

OLD-WORLD BEERS

Although HammerHeart's beers are produced with great skill and are based on long-standing brewing traditions, it's not the kind of beer menu that is going to move large volumes in the outer-suburban setting of Lino Lakes. The area is probably better suited for macro beers than craft, much less completely foreign styles. "What we do is simply not for everybody. There will be people who come in and are horrified by it. I get it; the first time I had smoked beer I was pretty shocked," Lunn says with a laugh. It's tough to walk the line between marketability and remaining true to HammerHeart's roots, but Lunn will never sell out. It's simply not in his spirit.

Lunn reflects, "Because we are such an unpopular beer style, it's kind of an uphill battle. But we can't be a brewery that has an old-school Viking/Celtic theme and make fucking hazy IPAs. What are we going to do? Talk about black metal and then say here's our pastry stout?" Instead, the taproom pours pints of minimally bitter IPAs and serves beers made with malt that was cured over an open beechwood fire—neither of which is popular by nature, but it's what Lunn does.

HammerHeart also sticks to its guns as a brewery grounded in one location. Limiting the brewing and distribution range to just a taproom location was a risk, but Lunn felt it was necessary in order to preserve the integrity of the brand. "We would make so much more money if we were a gypsy brewery," he says. A gypsy brewery is one that has no set home, but instead travels to brew on other breweries' systems. (Notably, the term is now recognized as an ethnic slur.) The lower overhead and greater distribution opportunities with gypsy brewing would increase

HammerHeart's margins, but the model would also preclude direct connection with consumers in a community gathering space. According to Lunn, the thing that "saved their ass" financially was sending hand-bottled beers to dedicated fans in such diverse locations as Kentucky, Illinois, and Quebec. A demand and respect for HammerHeart's beer styles exist, as folks from all over the country and world come to the taproom and have HammerHeart beer shipped out of state.

HammerHeart occupies a special niche in the Minnesota and American craft beer markets. From its beer styles to its cabin-style taproom, the HammerHeart experience is one of a kind. While the beer might be different than what most craft drinkers are accustomed to, the taproom still offers all the features of a third place. If the notion of a smoked beer intimidates you, I invite you to open yourself up to a new flavor and great conversation at the HammerHeart bar.

A variety of handmade tap handles add to the woodsy Norse aesthetic.

BEERS TO KNOW

Flaming Longship: A mildly smoked brew in the Scotch ale/wee heavy style.

Olaf the Stout: Named after the Norwegian king who ended the pagan era in Norway, Olaf the Stout is a dark, rye stout hopped with cascade hops and aged in oak.

Stjørdal: Norwegian-style alderwood-smoked stjørdalsøl.

Thor's Imperial Porter: A smoked hot pepper imperial porter.

FAIR STATE BREWING COOPERATIVE

MINNESOTA'S FIRST COOPERATIVELY OWNED BREWERY

Minneapolis, Minnesota
Opened: September 2014
Barrels produced (2019): 11,321; 10th largest in state by production
The Team: Evan Sallee, president and CEO
Niko Tonks, head brewer
Matt Hauck, director of operations

COLLEGE BEGINNINGS

Minnesota's ninth-largest brewery by production was started by someone who was known as the guy who had "random beer fermenting under his bed in college." It's the perfect story of the ragtag, MacGyver-type scientist-turned-professional that represents what craft beer is for many Americans.

As an eighteen-year-old freshman at Carleton College in Northfield, Evan Sallee was pursuing his homebrewing hobby while also playing for the school rugby team, where he got to know teammate Niko Tonks. The pair lived together during and after college and eventually began homebrewing together. Together with Macalester College rugby player Matt Hauck, the three would go on to cofound Fair State Brewing Cooperative.

At the time, the friends didn't envision opening a brewery together. Based on my own college experience, I can only assume they were more focused on the beer than on the entrepreneurial potential. After graduation, Sallee, Tonks, and Hauck each went their separate ways to pursue graduate degrees and professional opportunities. Sallee attended law school at Northwestern University in Illinois, Hauck entered a graduate program at the University of Minnesota, and Tonks earned a master's degree at the University of Texas at Austin.

After securing his master's degree, Tonks started but then left a PhD program. In a 2015 interview with *The Growler*, he recalled,

Get your beer here at the Fair State Brewing Cooperative taproom in Minneapolis.

"I realized it's more or less impossible to get a job as a PhD in the humanities. And that if I had gotten one, it would have driven me completely nuts." He realized, instead, that what he wanted to do was brew beer professionally. So he started cold-emailing local breweries looking for work—even offering to work for free.

Tonks landed a gig at Live Oak Brewing Company in Austin, Texas. Sallee regards Live Oak as one of the best breweries in the nation. The Texas operation—started by homebrewers like themselves—is known for its decoction mashing, a style of brewing that draws out and highlights complex malt flavors. The method lends itself to brewing fantastic Czech- and German-style brews.

Sallee and Hauck went down to visit Tonks in Austin, and the trio drank beers together at Black Star Brewing Cooperative, completely unaware how much that place would change their futures. Black Star, which opened in September 2010, is the world's first cooperatively owned and worker-managed brewpub. With the taproom bill having just passed in Minnesota, a light bulb went off for the three friends. Sallee recalls that they knew that being able to have taprooms would be "a game changer for this state. We knew we had to do it now or forever hold our peace. So, perhaps foolishly, we decided to just do it."

THE COOPERATIVE MODEL

Building a brewery within the cooperative model was relatively unheard of when Sallee, Hauck, and Tonks decided to make that leap, and more than five years after Fair State opened its doors, it still isn't common, especially in Minnesota. Fair State was the first in the state, and it has since been followed only by Broken Clock Brewing Cooperative, also in Minneapolis.

Running a business as a cooperative carries an additional layer of complication for the owners compared to using a more traditional model. There are members to connect with and programs to build out for them like bottle releases and happy hours, bank loans to negotiate under the unorthodox financing structure, and an extra layer of information to communicate to consumers.

Despite such challenges, Minnesota has a long history of cooperatives, including multinational companies like Land O'Lakes and small neighborhood grocery stores, and at the time it was home to the most cooperatively owned businesses in the country. Sallee, Hauck, and Tonks knew that Minnesotans were already receptive to both the business model and craft beer, so they took the long shot at bringing the two together.

In a 2015 interview with *The Growler*, head brewer Tonks said, "The cooperative model appealed to us initially as a way to allow beer enthusiasts to be involved in the formation of a brewery. People really care about their local breweries, a rare and wonderful thing in a world of globalized capitalism, and I think it makes the brewing industry a

"I THINK THERE ARE WAYS IN WHICH THE COOPERATIVE BUSINESS MODEL CAN BE EXPANDED UPON AND WAYS THAT WE CAN SERVE AS EXAMPLES TO OTHER BUSINESSES THAT YOU CAN BUILD A SUCCESSFUL, GROWING, AND VIBRANT BUSINESS, AND YOU CAN DO IT IN A FAIR WAY, AND YOU CAN DO IT WHILE HAVING YOUR CONSUMERS BE ACTUAL STAKEHOLDERS IN THE BUSINESS. AND YOU DON'T HAVE TO BE CONFINED TO BEING A NEIGHBORHOOD BREWERY OR BEING A PARTICULAR TYPE OF BREWERY."

—EVAN SALLEE, FAIR STATE BREWING COOPERATIVE

Photos of Fair State's member-owners are featured on the taproom walls.

natural fit for the co-op model." Sallee echoes this sentiment: "People are so bought into their local brewery, but they aren't literally bought in."

The three friends introduced Fair State Brewing Cooperative in March 2013 at a "coming-out party" in the Miller Textile Building in Northeast Minneapolis (now home of HeadFlyer Brewing). In addition to revealing the branded signage for their brewery, they offered a handful of homebrews "to show people we wouldn't be making completely terrible beer," remembers Sallee. For $200 per individual or $300 for a household, you could buy your own little slice of the brewery. In addition to warm fuzzy feelings, member-owners get to vote on the direction of the business, give input into which beers are made, gain special access to beers and events, and earn financial returns in the form of beer discounts and eventual patronage refunds.

The attendees at the original coming-out party were the first folks invited to become members of the new cooperative brewery. Fifty people signed on. Then, those first members brought the cofounders into their homes for similarly styled monthly gatherings to proselytize to more potential members—and it worked. Before Fair State even opened, it had 250 members. “People had a lot of faith in us,” Sallee remembers, “and that was really astonishing to me.” Five years later, in 2020, the brewery has 1,700 member-owners. Sallee doesn’t think there will be a plateau to membership as long as the brewery continues to reevaluate the membership program and adapt to its growing and changing constituency.

OPENING THE TAPROOM

During the early period of business development, Tonks was working at Sociable Cider Werks in Minneapolis, Sallee had passed the bar and was practicing law, and Hauck was working in social services by providing employment counseling. Once they had secured enough funding and a location for the brewery/taproom, it took about half a year to build out the Fair State space on Central Avenue in Minneapolis. The location came about through a group with a similar mindset: the NorthEast Investment Cooperative. The NEIC encourages residents to “invest financially to collectively buy, rehab, and manage commercial and residential property in Northeast Minneapolis.” Much like Fair State, NEIC works toward multiple bottom lines: sustainable economic development, local ownership of community assets, and a modest return on members’ investment.

The Fair State owners did much of the work to build the brewery and taproom on their own. Although members did help, the team did not want to take advantage of anybody’s eagerness to pitch in without being able to pay them a substantive wage. That was just the beginning of the men putting their social and economic ideologies to work.

The Fair State taproom is a modest 1,500 square feet of hardwood floors and café-style seating. Large windows face a bustling, multicultural Central Avenue. Near the front door is a bulletin board highlighting community events. Photos of the member-owners are on display in a collage-style mural on the wall opposite a bar that stretches half the length of the space. A long hallway through a back door leads to a beer garden, a cozy space filled with umbrella-covered picnic tables. A community garden grows hop bines near an active cornhole court adjacent to the alleyway.

Fair State's taproom is a gathering place for the community. This concept had played a central part in the cofounders' original decision to build a cooperative brewery with a dedicated membership. The cooperative offers the opportunity for the public to engage more deeply with the brewery. Sallee notes that breweries are a unique space in American culture for their ability to build social capital. With the founders holding degrees in public policy, American studies, and political science, it's no surprise that theories of social and civic engagement are part of the business plan. In addressing social capital, Sallee is referencing Robert D. Putnam, a political scientist whose book *Bowling Alone* argues that Americans have been engaging with social

The Fair State taproom is relatively small considering the brewery's production volume, but it is a popular community gathering space.

organizations (parent-teacher associations, Kiwanis clubs, bowling leagues, and the like) less and less since the 1950s, which has an impact on the function of our democracy. Those weekly gatherings of social groups once functioned as an important scene for civic discussion and engagement among neighbors.

Similar to the idea of taprooms as a third place, Sallee believes that breweries are a new social organization where people can engage with their community. "Declining social capital has been a big trend in America," he says. "I think that breweries are serving as a new kind of place for people to interact and connect with their communities." Fair State is modeled to function in this way, and Sallee acknowledges that other breweries are bringing communities together, too.

TAKE OVER THE TWIN CITIES, TAKE OVER THE WORLD

What brought Fair State from a humble taproom operating under a never-been-used business model to one of the largest beer producers in Minnesota? Sallee turns it back on the people: "We've got an incredibly talented team here who are really passionate about what they do. We try very hard as a business to attract talented people and reward them. We try to treat people fairly and equitably, and I think that shows in the way that we're able to attract and keep people." A focus on labor rights and sustainable business practices rings through in just about everything Fair State does: business model, construction, hiring, and employee retention.

Having a great team can set up any business for success, but having good beer and a welcoming space doesn't hurt, either. "We've always been committed from day one to making extremely good beer," Sallee continues, "but a lot of places locally make extremely good beer. I always say that having good beer is just the price of entry, and you have to be able to do everything else really well around that. One of our core values is improvement, and we try to consistently improve what we're doing. ... I think we've gotten really good at bringing out new beers and being able to produce really high-quality beer across a broad variety of styles." Achieving this standard and breadth of quality is key to operating a successful taproom in a competitive market. If breweries hope to serve as a community meeting ground, they need to have something for everyone. And, like Sallee says, good beer is simply the price of entry.

Clearly, Fair State's commitment to quality paid off. It wasn't long before the brewery was pushing production limits in its Minneapolis facility. The 2,000-barrel capacity of the taproom brewery simply could not keep up with the demand of its eager members and the public. In September 2016, just two years after opening, Fair State Brewing Cooperative announced plans to expand to a production-brewing facility in St. Paul.

The estimated $2 million, 40,000-square-foot facility in the St. Anthony Park neighborhood is now home to the Fair State offices and the majority of its production. Following state law, all beer produced in the St. Paul facility must be packaged to sell off-site. The beer served in the taproom must be brewed in the immediately adjacent brewhouse. The expansion, Sallee says, "changed just about everything with how we needed to do business." Fair State had to hire many more people, and the move allowed them to mature as a business: "Before that, you could hardly get our beer outside Northeast Minneapolis."

While the production facility became the primary site of financial growth for Fair State, it also served as a continuation for and expansion of the philosophies that built their Northeast Minneapolis taproom. Sallee comments, "Our vision is to find better and more ways for the co-op model to resonate outside the confines of our taproom. The taproom is the mother ship: it is the core of what we do and how we do it and how we interact with people because we can own every aspect of that interaction." The core support for Fair State comes from people and businesses near the taproom, but Fair State continues to explore ways to build community beyond its neighborhood and, in turn, ways to evolve the business.

The business continues to evolve, not just in physical growth but also in its management of and relation to its staff. On September 9, 2020, Fair State announced that it would be the first microbrewery in

The beer garden at Fair State is a sunny oasis amidst its Northeast Minneapolis neighborhood.

the country to unionize. The staff requested the brewery voluntarily recognize their union the day before, and ownership—in conjunction with the member-owner board of directors—quickly moved to do so. Sallee wrote in his announcement on the Fair State website, "We founded this cooperative on democratic principles, and this is the next natural step in our push to show that fair and democratic workplaces can thrive. ... We have always been about pushing boundaries in the name of brewing excellent beer and building a fairer state of business, and our team is ready for the challenge." A few, larger, breweries preceded Fair State in unionizing, including Schell's in New Ulm, Headless Mumby in Olympia, Washington, and Anchor Brewing in San Francisco, California.

Every year in Minnesota seems to bring new trends in craft beer styles or changes in how breweries conduct business. For years prior to the taproom bill, brewers built their businesses around the production and distribution model, and they focused on consistent flagship brews to establish brand loyalty. Then, with the advent of taprooms beginning

Pils is one of several classic beer styles served up by Fair State.

in 2011, brewery owners could create a hybrid approach. Going forward, it might be a different story. In Sallee's view, "a lot of breweries are opening in more neighborhood-focused models, and I think that is going to continue."

The neighborhood model is at the heart of what Fair State does. Sallee recalls, "That's how we got started. It's a much more sustainable way to start your business." We see this trend with the growing rate of breweries popping up in the suburbs and outstate Minnesota over the metro area's open rates. Of the twenty-four breweries that opened in 2019, two were in the Twin Cities, another eight in the metro area, and fourteen beyond.

Sallee sees continued opportunity for craft beer growth in Minnesota. "There are so many cities and places that just don't have breweries yet," he points out, "so I think there's a ton of ceiling for breweries to continue to spread throughout the state. There have been so many amazing stories about so many smaller towns that experienced an exodus, and a brewery coming in and helping to reverse that trend to provide a focal point for people to come and interact."

BEERS TO KNOW

Mirror Universe: "Mirror Universe is a dank, double dry-hopped hazy IPA brewed with wheat, oats, and tons of hops. With the critical success of Fair State's first hazy IPA, Spirit Føul, followed by Mirror Universe, the co-op has secured a reputation as producers of balanced and high-quality hazy beer, a style that is wildly popular with consumers." 7% ABV, 33 IBU

Pils: "Pils is a dry, German-style pilsner with a grassy hop aroma and a crisp finish. The simplicity of pilsners means there's no room for masking errors with crazy adjuncts or new techniques. This is a straightforward and delicious beer, perfectly made. ... Pils is also a staff favorite, to the extent that we affectionately refer to ourselves as Pils*nerds*." 5.1% ABV, 40 IBU

Roselle: "Roselle is a floral kettle sour infused with hibiscus, which lends the beer its citrus aromas and flavors and its red hue. Beer nerds appreciate the floral hibiscus infusion. Folks who are new to beer are pleasantly surprised by a beer that tastes tart, fruity, and floral. Roselle was one of the first beers we put into cans back in 2016, and that longevity has deeply associated the beer with the Fair State brand. It's a beer our customers love, and it's a beer we love." 5.7% ABV, 18 IBU

AWARDS TO KNOW

Fair State has won several awards for its label designs and was named "Best Brewery" by *City Pages* in 2018. Mirror Universe, Pils, and Vienna Lager all made that publication's list of "40 Best Beers in Minnesota" in 2019.

2018 *The Growler* "Kind-of-a-Big-Deal" Award: Mirror Universe, Best Hazy or New England IPA

2018 *The Growler* "Kind-of-a-Big-Deal" Award: Roselle, Best Kettle Sour

2019 Brewers Cup Awards: BFDP, First Place, Sour Barrel-Aged Beers

2019 Brewers Cup Awards: LÄCTOBÄC, Third Place, Wild & Sour Ales

SURLY BREWING COMPANY

MINNESOTA'S TAPROOM TRAILBLAZER AND LEGENDARY DESTINATION BREWERY

Minneapolis, Minnesota
Brewery opened (Brooklyn Center): January 2006
Taproom opened (Minneapolis): December 2014
Barrels produced (2019): 92,292; 3rd largest in state by production
The Team: Omar Ansari, owner and founder

THE BIRTH OF SURLY

In many ways, Surly Brewing Company paved the way for the modern craft beer boom in Minnesota. Before Surly opened, the growing popularity of regional breweries distributing to the Midwest primed Minnesotans' interest in craft beer. Summit and Schell's offered some proof of concept that a Minnesota-based craft brewery could succeed. But Surly is the business, and Omar Ansari the person, Minnesotans can point to as the most significant contributor to our current craft beer climate.

When Ansari launched Surly in 2006, it was the first new brewery to open in Minnesota in two decades (excluding brewpubs). The son of entrepreneurial immigrants—his father from Pakistan, his mother from Germany—Ansari built his brewery in a building in suburban Brooklyn Center that was, until that point, his parents' industrial abrasives factory. Speaking of his father, Ansari told the *Star Tribune* in 2016, "The American dream was very much a real thing to my parents, coming from other countries. So for him to see this place [the brewery] open meant everything to me."

The little Brooklyn Center brewery grew in popularity—and grew and grew. Along with his head brewer, Todd Haug, Ansari built a following unlike any we've seen from other Minnesota breweries. That group of followers became Surly Nation, and they are heavily credited with the passage of the taproom bill—so much so that it is often referred to as the "Surly Bill."

Surly owner Omar Ansari helped to revolutionize the craft beer scene in Minnesota.

After starting to homebrew in his garage in 1994, Ansari pursued a formal brewing education with an internship at Michigan's New Holland Brewing. Haug, meanwhile, got his start in the business at Summit before moving on to Rock Bottom Brewery in Minneapolis and helping to turn around that brewpub's reputation. The two eventually joined forces to build what would become one of Minnesota's largest operating breweries.

Ansari was inspired to start his own craft brewery after he struggled to find great craft beer in Minnesota, a fact that made him a little—wait for it—surly. By February 2006, Ansari and Haug sold their first keg of Surly beer out of the Brooklyn Center abrasives factory, making Surly the third production brewery operating in Minnesota at the time (following Summit and Schell's).

Ansari's next great inspiration came when he attended the 2008 Craft Brewers Conference in San Diego. While there, he visited the new Stone Brewing World Bistro and Gardens in nearby Escondido. Stone, which is now the ninth-largest craft brewery in the country, changed the game for craft beer. The brewery's World Bistro and Garden facility, opened in November 2006, spans 8,500 square feet plus a one-acre beer garden. In what was a highly innovative move at the time, Stone put an emphasis on offering high-quality food to elevate its beer offerings while creating an inviting environment for customers.

Seeing the space transformed Ansari's understanding of what a brewery taproom and craft beer experience could be. He recalls thinking, *Are you kidding? Look at what craft beer has become.* He adds, "Something changed at that moment for me." He came to understand that craft beer could offer an elevated flavor experience for the general consumer, and that a taproom could be so much more than a simple beer hall.

Unfortunately, at the time, Ansari couldn't build something like Stone's lavish taproom in Minnesota, where breweries were prohibited by law from serving beer in a taproom. But Ansari also knew that something had to change for Surly. The demand for its beer would soon outgrow the capacity of the Brooklyn Center facility. By December 2008, Surly reached 3,500 barrels of production, putting it beyond the permitted limit for selling growlers. Before too long, if growth continued at such a pace, the brewery would hit the production cap for self-distribution—25,000 barrels—which would require it to start working with wholesale beer distributors and therefore take a huge hit on its profit margins. (Surly hit the cap in 2013, when it brewed 28,971 barrels of beer.) To maintain the same level of profitability, the brewery would have to jump from 25,000 self-distributed barrels to brewing 45,000 barrels annually distributed through a wholesaler. Neither Ansari nor Haug wanted to grow Surly at that rate just to have a bigger production brewery. As solely a distribution brewery, they would lose connection with their customers, and neither wanted to sacrifice that. Something needed to change.

TAKING IT TO THE CAPITOL

Already motivated by what he had seen at Stone Brewing, the next big moment of inspiration for Ansari came when Jim Mott, a Surly employee from its earliest days, returned from a trip to Europe and

Patrons regularly pack Surly's huge, beer hall–style taproom to enjoy the brewery's wide range of beer and food offerings. *Photo courtesy of Surly Brewing Company*

brought with him a brochure from the expansive Stiegl Brewery in Austria. It was the final push Ansari needed to fight to change the way beer worked in Minnesota. He recalls looking at the brochure and thinking, "If we could sell someone a glass of beer—maybe if we could do *that*—it would be altogether different." If he could build a bigger brewery where people could congregate and drink their beers, it would be great for his business and for the Minnesota beer community. And all he needed to do was change Minnesota's laws and overturn its long-standing restrictive attitudes. "I could see it working," Ansari recalls, "that we would get this law changed so we could build a new brewery and bring this piece that Minnesota just never had: the beer hall piece."

So, as Jess Fleming wrote in the *Pioneer Press* following the opening of Surly's new brewery and taproom in December 2014, "Ansari set out to change the law, a challenge many had undertaken, but none had accomplished." The article further noted that a local politician had even recommended to Ansari that he consider relocating to Wisconsin, given the seemingly insurmountable obstacle of a powerful liquor lobby in Minnesota determined to preserve the status quo.

Ansari recalls the process of getting the bill passed as a roller coaster filled with "dirty politics." "It was super emotional and really hard," he says.

As the date approached when the state legislature was going to vote on the bill, Ansari unleashed his secret weapon: the Surly Nation. The brewery had been holding its fans at bay throughout the process of getting the bill to the floor of the legislature. When it came time for the legislators to vote, Surly let the fans loose. "No one counted on the level of support Surly's die-hard fans would provide," Fleming wrote in 2014. "They called and wrote state legislators. They testified. They tweeted. They signed petitions." Thankfully, after all that hard work, the taproom bill was signed into Minnesota state law in May 2011.

DESTINATION BEER

Ansari's vision to open a welcoming and attractive destination brewery took a major step toward reality in late October 2013 when ground was broken at the site in Minneapolis's Prospect Park neighborhood. Fourteen months later, in December 2014, Surly welcomed its first guests into its $35 million brewery and taproom, and a new era in Minnesota craft beer was born. As Brian Kaufenberg wrote in an article for *The Growler* celebrating the opening of the expansive facility, "Surly's destination brewery is more than just an impressive structure—it's an extension of the Surly culture that birthed a 'Nation' of craft beer drinkers who rallied around the idea that a full-flavored beer should never be hard to find."

The new brewery was so much more than just a taproom. Ringing in at an impressive 50,000 square feet, the two-story complex features multiple restaurants, a brewhouse, a gift shop, and a massive taproom. Enormous tables and benches stretch from the copper brewing equipment looming behind a large glass wall to enormous windows on the other end that lead out to the beer garden, a lovely outdoor space nestled within the brewery's industrial surroundings. The beer hall's kitchen serves refined bar food like chilaquiles, smoked mushrooms, and barley soup. Upstairs, an event hall and casual—and delicious—pizza restaurant round out the space.

Just as things were really taking off, the brewery—and the entire Minnesota craft beer scene—was shaken by the announcement that longtime brewer Todd Haug was leaving Surly. He headed to 3 Floyds in

The Surly taproom spills over into an expansive patio and garden areas. *Photo courtesy of Surly Brewing Company*

Chicago. Although Haug had been Surly's brewer since the beginning, he had no ownership stake, and so he set off for new opportunities. Meanwhile, Surly continued to expand its empire.

In the summer of 2016, Surly launched an outdoor concert series at its Festival Field behind the brewery building. Held in partnership with Minneapolis's iconic First Avenue club, the summer series kicked off with a sold-out show by Edward Sharpe and the Magnetic Zeros. Subsequent years featured such top acts as Father John Misty, Spoon, Courtney Barnett, Gary Clark Jr., and the Hold Steady, among others. In 2019, Surly welcomed its most massive music lineup yet, with headliners including Lord Huron, Tame Impala, Ben Folds, Violent Femmes, Shakey Graves, and Nathaniel Rateliff & the Night Sweats. *Minnesota Monthly* named it the "Summer of Surly."

Another popular Surly tradition is the annual Darkness Day. First introduced in 2006, Darkness is a Russian imperial stout that garnered a lot of attention from craft beer lovers and led to people lining up for hours for a chance to purchase the new releases in the series each September. Darkness Day, originally held at Surly's Brooklyn Center facility, is a daylong music and beer festival that attracts thousands. The annual release party got so large that in 2018 Surly relocated it to the Somerset Amphitheater, across the border in Wisconsin. Ansari announced in early 2020 that Surly was canceling that year's festival—not because of the COVID-19 pandemic that would soon bring all such gatherings to a halt, but because of the Minnesota law that prohibits Surly from selling beer in growlers (since it produces more than 20,000 barrels per year), thus limiting its ability to share the popular Darkness.

GRASSROOTS

Despite Surly's massive growth and high profile, Ansari still claims the success of the brewery—and the beer scene it produced—is based in grassroots energy.

Although he has a somewhat cynical perspective on the nature of consumerism in this country, Ansari has held firm in his belief that people truly care about where and by whom their beer is brewed. When he worked at his parents' industrial abrasives factory, he says, "I was keenly aware that people really don't give a fuck where their stuff comes from. Everyone complains about China this and Walmart that, but that's where they shop. It's cheaper. ... Beer is one of those things that's left that people really do care about. They want to know the brewer and they want to see the place."

Ansari says Surly's success all started with passionate customers. He remembers one such customer who approached him during a Surly event years ago at an Old Chicago restaurant. She told Ansari how much she loved Bender, Surly's brown ale, and that she would always buy a pint of it for anybody she saw order a Newcastle Brown Ale at the bar. Ansari was surprised and flattered, to which she responded, "People should be drinking local beer—this beer is way better. Why wouldn't I do that?" Ansari says, "Those are the people who brought us from a two-

Food and beer come together in a flavor extravaganza at Surly. *Photo courtesy of Surly Brewing Company*

person start-up thirteen years ago to a company of four hundred people. Those are the people who got the law changed, and those are the people who are responsible for 180 breweries in the state."

Ansari doesn't know where Surly, or the industry, will go from here. In 2019, for the first time in its history, Surly brewed fewer barrels than it did the year before. That doesn't mean a loss for the brewing giant, however. "At the end of the day," Ansari notes, "you pay your bills with your profit and not with your number of barrels." Surly has diversified its revenue streams beyond selling beer at its taproom and in bars and liquor stores around town. The food and festivals continue to expand the craft beer experience beyond anything Minnesotans had previously imagined. By creating a space where people celebrate, volunteer, party, and commune—and by developing an innovative and diverse line of beers—Surly has done much to pave the way for the craft beer industry in Minnesota.

As this book went to press, there were significant developments at Surly. Their front- and back-of-house employees announced their intent to unionize on August 31. Two days later, on September 2, Surly announced that it would close the beer hall indefinitely starting on November 2, citing the financial impact of the COVID-19 pandemic. When asked the definition of "indefinitely" in this context, owner Omar Ansari told the *Star Tribune*, "I guess when COVID is over. But I'll be honest and say that I haven't had a lot of hope in the last few weeks. Until people can gather—because that's the way that this place is designed—we can't keep losing money."

BEERS TO KNOW

Furious IPA: A lightning-in-a-bottle, punch-you-in-the-face, hop-bomb of an IPA. "The beer that built Surly. Aggressively hopped and citrusy, but with a chewy, caramel malt backbone." 6.7% ABV, 100 IBU

More than just a spectacular taproom, Surly also produces an innovative lineup of tasty beers. *Photo courtesy of Surly Brewing Company*

Abrasive: "A massive dose of Citra hops launches our legendary double IPA (Minnesota's first, and a nod to our abrasives factory origin) into the hophead stratosphere." 9.2% ABV, 100 IBU

Axe Man: "Double dry-hopping with Citra and Mosaic hops creates this world-renowned IPA's intense tropical fruit and citrus aromas. Brewed with Golden Promise malt, this beer finishes rich and dry." This IPA was first brewed in collaboration with Amager Brewery in Denmark and was originally called Todd the Axe Man after the first head brewer, Todd Haug. 7.2% ABV, 65 IBU

Darkness: The beer that launched an entire festival. Surly's "massive Russian imperial stout contains waves of chocolate, coffee, cherry, raisin, and toffee, plus a nontraditional dose of aromatic hops." Since 2015, the annual release also comes in a barrel-aged version. 10.3% ABV

Xtra Citra Pale Ale: A session pale ale. "Bursting with Citra hop flavor and tropical, citrusy notes, this incredibly approachable pale ale showcases Surly's bright side." 4.5% ABV, 50 IBU

AWARDS TO KNOW

Surly has been named among the top craft brewers in the state, the country, and the world by such sources as the Brewers Association, BeerAdvocate, RateBeer, *Thrillist,* and more. Surly beers have also been recognized by both national and local experts.

2016 Great American Beer Festival: Barrel-Aged Darkness, Gold Medal, Wood- and Barrel-Aged Strong Stout category

2017 RateBeer: Surly Darkness, Top Beer

2018 BeerAdvocate: Todd the Axe Man, Best American IPA

2019 Brewers Cup Awards: Xtra Citra Pale Ale, Second Place, Pale Ales

2019 *The Growler* "Kind-of-a-Big-Deal" Award: Axe Man, Best IPA

2019 *The Growler* "Kind-of-a-Big-Deal" Award: Pentagram, Best Sour

2019 RateBeer: Xtra Citra Pale Ale, Best English-Style Pale Ale

BANG BREWING

MINNESOTA'S FIRST ALL-ORGANIC BREWERY

St. Paul, Minnesota
Opened: September 2013
Barrels produced (2019): 243; 135th largest in state by production
The Team: Jay Boss Febbo, co-owner and co-brewer
Sandy Boss Febbo, co-owner and co-brewer

BIG IMPACT WITH A SMALL FOOTPRINT

Every decision made by Sandy and Jay Boss Febbo, the wife-and-husband duo behind Bang Brewing, is driven by the goal of making a big impact while maintaining a small footprint. Their organic, sustainably minded brewery is the first of its kind in Minnesota, and with every pint poured, this little St. Paul brewery is proving that it's possible to be both discerning in your choice of beverage and kind to the planet.

Opening a brewery is a tough enough undertaking in itself, and trying to run the business in the most environmentally sustainable way possible only brings additional burden, as it is more expensive and more time consuming. So why do it? Sandy answers, "It's how we're wired: how we cook, how we garden, how we feed our dogs. It comes from an environmental stewardship point of view." The couple simply would never consider running their business any other way. Sustainable and organic living is what they do. Not only are the Boss Febbos committed to sticking to their values as they pursue their passion, they also want their brewery to serve as an example for the industry and to encourage more brewery owners to follow the sustainable model.

Sandy and Jay don't make a single decision in the brewery without considering the environmental implications. Their building design, ingredient sourcing, and packaging all work toward zero waste and minimizing environmental impact. In fact, this approach requires minimalism in all areas of business, sometimes at the cost of certain bells and whistles. For example, Bang has yet to open a

Sustainability and maintaining a small footprint are guiding principles at Bang Brewing.

merchandise shop because doing so would mean having to take on the additional work of sourcing earth-friendly suppliers, ink shops, and embroiderers to produce Bang-branded clothing and gear. With a staff of just seven—including the two owners—side projects like that just aren't feasible.

Even without branded beanies and T-shirts, Bang is showing the craft beer industry that organic brewing is a viable business model. "It still kind of blows my mind that we are the only brewery in Minnesota that uses only organic and sustainably farmed ingredients," Sandy says. "We don't have the economy of scale, but we are proving that it's possible."

Part of the Bang philosophy of "big impact with a small footprint" is the concept of the "quadruple bottom line," an expansion on the "triple bottom line" approach to accounting that encourages businesses to consider social and environmental profits and losses in addition to the financial ones. According to the Oregon-based 3E Strategies, the fourth bottom line in the quadruple model looks at intentional work by an organization to help improve the environment and society: "The fourth bottom line provides an opportunity for companies to focus on creating products and business models that are intentionally designed to improve the health of the planet and community wellbeing."

In order to run their business on this model, the Boss Febbos often end up reverse engineering projects to be environmentally responsible as well as profitable. It's not an easy way to do business, but it's value driven, and that is what matters to the Boss Febbos. In addition to the brewery's building design and landscaping, Bang has taken on a host of additional sustainability measures, including installing energy-efficient brewing equipment and appliances, packaging off-sale beer in returnable bottles, and working toward zero waste.

EFFICIENCY IN THE ROUND

Bang Brewing operates out of a 1,300-square-foot brewery fabricated from a circular grain bin by Geoffrey Warner of Alchemy Architects. Choosing a round building was deliberate: the circle is a highly efficient shape, which minimizes Bang's footprint. As much as possible, the equipment and furniture are on wheels to allow the space to accommodate both brewing and drinking. About fifty people can fit inside the taproom, but the beautiful sprawling patio triples that capacity. With a year-round firepit and pollinator-friendly rain garden, the scene is a serene urban setting.

Sandy and Jay spent two years scoping out a location for their brewery in their hometown of St. Paul. They struggled to find a space with a small footprint that also met local ordinance requirements for microbreweries. Their efforts to work with the City of St. Paul to change zoning restrictions to allow for a microbrewery in the central corridor were unsuccessful. All the spaces that fulfilled their small footprint requirement were storefronts with wood floors and basements, which simply could not support a brewhouse.

Before long, the couple knew every street in St. Paul. They also knew that for what it would cost to do a buildout in an existing building, they could build their own space on the mostly abandoned industrial Capp Road.

In late 2010 or early 2011, Jay and Sandy reached out to Alchemy Architects, located on Raymond Avenue, just a few blocks from Bang's future site. They had been impressed with the firm's prefab small-space residential designs in Wisconsin—a line of homes now called the weeHouse. "They're super material savvy, environmentally savvy, and their design is fantastic," Sandy says of Alchemy. "They espouse working within budgets. We just needed that brain on this project."

Bang and Alchemy Architects went through several design iterations together. The first round was a custom build that blew the budget; the second was a prefab space based on pole barns that was larger and still more expensive. In the third round, Alchemy said to the Boss Febbos, "You don't like squares, and you don't like rectangles, and you want a small footprint. Grain bin?" It was a light bulb moment. The circular shape allowed them to keep the business—the brewhouse—on the perimeter of the space, while leaving the center open and available for any use. With the passage of the taproom bill in 2011, that space would become essential for the business, allowing room for tables where customers could enjoy the brews. Sandy adds that the grain bin "has a happy-accident awesome visual tie back to farms." With the brewery's focus on organic ingredients and responsible sourcing, it is fitting that its building draws directly from an architectural staple of a midwestern farm. There is no escaping the interconnectedness of farming and brewing in the Bang brewhouse.

In September 2013, the taproom quietly opened. Sandy and Jay told only their friends and family about the opening, and they let the news spread by word of mouth. They decided to call the brewery "Bang" as an esoteric reference to Jay's software engineering method of titling his homebrew recipes (in some scripts, the exclamation point, or *bang*, is used to tell the program to run a certain command) as well as Sandy's interest in typography from her days as an advertising professional. In an interview with *The Growler* in 2013 just before the brewery opened, Sandy explained that while many people know that *bang* is a typographical term for an exclamation point, it also "represents an emotion and an intent."

Bang's grain bin taproom is a distinctive and purposeful setting for a brewery. It is also surrounded by plantings of prairie grasses and wildflowers.

GOING OUTDOORS

The brewery and taproom were just one side of the Boss Febbos' dreams. They also envisioned an outdoor space that would not only contribute to local ecology but also work to educate patrons on environmental stewardship. Rather than paving a patio for additional seating, the Boss Febbos aimed for a natural patio space.

The original plan was to landscape the patio with barley. They were so excited by the tiny growth they saw early on, Sandy recalls: "We were the biggest city kids when that barley started to sprout." Then the spring rains came. Parking lot runoff swept away all those germinated seeds. The aspiring landscapers tried again the next year, and once again the spring rains foiled their plans. They realized, *We get all this stormwater, so we need to do something about it.* The Boss Febbos reached out to the Capitol Region Watershed District (CRWD), a government organization dedicated to connecting land, water, and community.

In November 2015, Bang, the CRWD, and the Ramsey County Soil and Water Conservation Division broke ground on a native prairie and rain garden project on the Boss Febbos' one-sixth-acre plot. They installed two multicelled rain gardens to capture the rainwater runoff from the parking lot. According to the CRWD, "While it may not be apparent to visitors at first glance, the rocks and grasses in the parking lot can catch and clean more than 100,000 gallons of stormwater runoff annually."

The resulting beer garden is a peaceful grassy space with picnic tables and a firepit. Patrons can tuck themselves away amongst the grasses to enjoy a semi-private slice of nature in the middle of an industrial district. The overhead pavilion and picnic tables, coupled with the firepit, create the shape of a bang, or exclamation point. "The best part about that garden design is the bang," says Sandy. It's a serendipitous finishing touch on a beautiful beer garden.

STRIVING FOR SUSTAINABLE BEER

Brewing beer solely with organic ingredients is no easy feat, given the challenges of ingredient sourcing. Nevertheless, Sandy and Jay have a well-rounded tap list that includes IPAs, porters, strong ales, and a farmhouse saison.

"The sourcing of our ingredients is a massively time consuming thing for us," notes Sandy. "It's one of our biggest challenges, and it's definitely one of our most rewarding successes that each year we have been able to gain access to more ingredient options. We have fewer options for ingredients than conventional brewers."

Because organic beer ingredients are so hard to come by, the brewers want to be sure to highlight those ingredients. They'll use their MOSH IPA to feature any new hop that comes in and learn more about it. MOSH—an initialism for Maris Otter, Single Hop—is a spinoff of the Single Malt and Single Hop, or SMaSH, style of brewing that allows each ingredient, specifically the malt and the hops, to stand out. Bang features Maris Otter malts and a rotating specialty hop to produce a clean beer that keeps the hop's flavor profile unobscured by additional ingredients.

The long picnic table in the beer garden ends at a circular fire pit, forming the shape of a bang!

In 2011, a new ingredient emerged in the market that would make brewing organic, sustainable beer far easier. The ingredient had actually been around for centuries but was not used for human consumption. Kernza, the trademark name for a type of wheatgrass, is a perennial grain with long roots, making it substantially more environmentally friendly than barley, wheat, rice, and other grains. Kernza made its debut on the beer scene in a 2016 collaboration between the Portland-based Hopworks Urban Brewery and Patagonia, with a pale ale called Long Root Ale. Just as it did with organic cotton in the 1990s, Patagonia invested in developing an eco-friendly alternative to other options on the market. These efforts to produce a Kernza beer also relied on work from the University of Minnesota's Forever Green Initiative—bringing the grain back home to the North Star State. Bang uses Kernza in several of its beers: Kernza Blonde Ale, Gold, KIPA (Kernza IPA), and FARM (Kernza Farmhouse Ale).

Despite the advances with Kernza, organic and sustainably produced ingredients remain difficult to come by for Bang Brewing. The folks at Bang still work tirelessly to discover new ingredients and source new materials. They even founded an Organic Brewers Alliance to serve as an open source network for ingredients and partnerships. The alliance is producing maps of organic breweries and producers. Maybe their work will make organic and sustainable brewing more widespread.

All of Bang's ales and lagers are 100 percent organic and made with sustainably farmed ingredients.

Sandy and Jay Boss Febbo recognize that they've accomplished something special, against the odds. "We're fiercely proud that we're still here," Sandy says. "Never a day passes that we aren't aware that we make our living six dollars at a time. The beer matters—that's what it's all about."

BEERS TO KNOW

Bang IPA: Hoppy strong ale. 7.0% ABV, 65 IBU

MOSH IPA: 100% organic single malt (Maris Otter) single hop (rotating)

Neat Sparkling Bitter: 4.9% ABV, 90 IBU

Nice Dark Ale: 100% organic STP Dark Ale. 6.5% ABV, 65 IBU

AWARDS TO KNOW

Bang has been named best taproom by the *Star Tribune* and has received several accolades for its green and water-conservation initiatives.

URBAN GROWLER BREWING COMPANY

MINNESOTA'S FIRST WOMAN-OWNED AND -OPERATED BREWERY

St. Paul, Minnesota
Opened: July 2014
Barrels produced (2019): 1,700; 36th largest in state by production
The Team: Deb Loch, master brewer and co-owner
Jill Pavlak, co-owner

PARTNERS IN LIFE, PARTNERS IN BEER

Urban Growler's story started like many breweries' stories: with a homebrewing hobby born of a desire to drink good beer. Owner and brewer Deb Loch recalls her beginnings: "In the nineties, there wasn't a lot of good beer [available in Minnesota] yet. There was Sierra Nevada, and we hoped Fat Tire would cross the river to our neck of the woods. Summit was just getting started, but [there was] not the breadth of craft beer that we have now." In response to the sparse market, she started making beer herself. "I started getting more and more obsessed about [homebrewing]. I started thinking about the next recipe, the next piece of equipment, how I was going to make improvements."

Eventually, the entrepreneurially minded homebrewer and her life/business partner, Jill Pavlak, traded in their successful, steady-income careers (in engineering and sales, respectively) and turned their beer-making avocation into a vocation.

Loch, the homebrewer and engineer, and Pavlak, the sales, social media, and restaurant professional, met for a first date in 2006 at the Happy Gnome, a burger joint in St. Paul (now closed) known for its craft beer selection. Two years later, they began considering a future that included a relationship as business partners as well. Pavlak and Loch had a feeling they would make a complementary team, bringing together both hard and soft skills: Pavlak is the people person and the connector; Loch is focused on science, finance, and sustainable business models. In contemplating what type of business to pursue together, they considered B&Bs and coffee shops until, finally—as they discussed it over pints of Loch's homebrews—the light bulb flickered on: a brewery.

Pavlak was on board right away, but Loch wasn't satisfied that "my partner enjoys my homebrews" met the criteria for professional qualifications. "What's easy at the homebrew level," Loch notes, "turns into a whole different project at the macro brew level." In fact, Loch calls herself the biggest roadblock to getting the business started: "I had a great career and had a hard time making the leap. Not that any of that was bad, but I was afraid." On top of all the challenges that come with starting a new business, Loch knew that, as a female *and* gay brewer, she and Pavlak would have to over-deliver on quality and expertise. Loch knew she needed to gain credibility in order to cut it in a demanding and competitive industry. But once Loch was "all in," Pavlak says, things took off from there.

Loch started by building some professional experience to back up her years of hard work and skill development as a hobbyist. She had already picked up a job at a homebrew supply store to pay for her homebrewing ingredients, and she got an internship at a brewpub in northern Wisconsin that used a seven-barrel system. Next, Loch headed to the University of California, Davis to obtain her masters in brewing. After completing her degree, Loch secured another internship—this time at St. Paul's Summit Brewing with its sixty-barrel system. Loch recalls, "I'm a hands-on person. I needed to feel it, touch it, live it, and have the crappy start-at-2:00 AM hours or work where the brewery is 110 degrees. And I still loved it. That was a sign."

Pavlak concurs. "That's when I knew this was for sure going to happen," she says. "She's in Minocqua, Wisconsin. And I'm in Minneapolis calling, checking in on her, and she's like, 'I'm in the brewery; it's 120 degrees. I'm covered in yeast and grain and sweat, and I've never been happier.' And I thought, *Okay, we're doing this.*"

Meanwhile, Pavlak quit her sales job and was putting in hours at the Longfellow Grill and Surdyk's liquor store, learning customer preferences and gaining industry insight. With Loch's impressive brewing résumé and Pavlak's restaurant expertise, the pair was

Jill Pavlak (left) and Deb Loch (right) set out to create a welcoming environment at Urban Growler in St. Paul.

beholden to no outside parties when it came time to open their own business. They could run this ship on their own—which also brought its challenges. "When we first opened," Loch recalls, "I was working one hundred hours a week brewing and then doing business stuff. I was forgetting to eat—and that doesn't happen very often."

Now, several years into the operation, the work is less grueling for the brewer. Loch and Pavlak are highly complimentary of their talented and supportive staff at Urban Growler. Loch's team includes four other brewers, and Urban Growler boasts a total staff of fifty during the busy season. The brewery still self-distributes, a business decision that, Pavlak says, allows them to be flexible and grow along with the industry. Loch adds, "We are flexible and nimble, and we adapt." The pair plans to have their beer in every liquor store in Minnesota by 2025.

BEER OASIS IN INDUSTRIAL ST. PAUL

When Loch and Pavlak began scouting locations to open their brewery in St. Paul, they had a wish list of specific attributes they were looking for: historical brick structure, south-facing beer garden, and ample parking. City ordinances required that the brewery operation be located in an industrial neighborhood. All these parameters, in addition to financial limitations, practically selected Urban Growler's taproom space for them. And, luckily, it was exactly what they had been dreaming of. An artist mocked up their vision in charcoal even before they found the space, and that drawing is a dead ringer for the taproom where it now hangs.

The gorgeous brick structure housed the City of St. Paul police force's horses back in the late 1800s and early 1900s. It then became a carriage repair shop, followed by the manufacturing site for Hart downhill skis and Northland professional hockey sticks, and other industrial uses. A brewery seems to fit right in with that diverse path through Minnesota history.

The Urban Growler patio is an oasis of a beer garden in summer. Pollinator-friendly flower boxes were planted in collaboration with the Wildflower Project, and the brewery celebrated the garden unveiling with their Mighty Buzz beer, a collaboration with Minnesota's own Mighty Axe Hops.

Inside, the taproom features a half-circle bar and a couple dozen restaurant-style high tops and tables. Visible behind the bar is the brewhouse, its shiny steel tanks always producing something new and fresh to fill your glass. The packaging and

From virtually any seat in the Urban Growler taproom, patrons can see how their beer is served—from brewhouse to pint glass. The brewery also has event spaces separate from the main taproom for hosting corporate events, weddings, musicians, and more.

storage operations are tucked in hidden rooms of the historical building, made to work with the building's existing layout.

The kitchen to the left of the bar bustles with activity, sending out full meals from a menu that offers far more than your brewery-standard pretzels and beef jerky. A large space in the back is available for rentals, and another smaller rentable space is situated upstairs, making Urban Growler a versatile and inviting site to host events.

Urban Growler's decision to include a full kitchen in its business model is one thing that differentiates it from most Minnesota taprooms. A restaurant brings a whole range of additional challenges and costs—such as space requirements, special permits, and additional equipment—not to mention the stress of high turnover and employee shortages common in the food-service industry. Operating a restaurant within a taproom essentially means operating two businesses, both of which have high start-up investments and high potential for failure.

On the other hand, a full food menu can be a perfect pairing for a craft brewery, giving patrons more than one reason to visit the taproom, thus capturing new customers and diversifying the revenue streams. It also means customers might linger longer, since they don't have to go elsewhere to get a bite to eat, and a little food in the stomach might allow them to try a couple more beers.

Pavlak and Loch decided the potential benefits outweighed the challenges. Still, Pavlak, the restaurant expert in the partnership, admits that the restaurant "is the hardest part of the entire business." It has taken a while to develop, but Pavlak adds, "we have a great chef, sous chef, and kitchen team."

The kitchen brings great benefit to the brand as well. Broadening Urban Growler's offerings to nonalcoholic and food options makes the space accessible to a wider range of people: families, non-drinkers, and folks who just want a bite to go along with their pint.

BY WOMEN, FOR EVERYONE

To be a woman in the brewing industry is rare enough. To also be queer makes for an even more uncommon combination, but it's not something either woman in the Urban Growler duo chooses to highlight. Loch and Pavlak strive to make gender and identity non-issues in their taproom. What they care about most is making sure their customers enjoy the food, beer, and connection in their brewery. "We truly believe we have more in common with people than we differ," Pavlak says. "We just want to be respected and known for great beer, fantastic food, and outstanding service."

The years when the pair began exploring opening a brewery were particularly contentious and divisive, socially and politically. "The Church was trying to fight gay marriage," Pavlak recalls. "We were both raised Catholic but not necessarily practicing, but it was very hurtful to hear. We just thought if people would sit down with us and have a beer, they'd realize we all have more in common than what divides us."

"So we opened this place. We want to bring people together through beer. We don't care how you vote, who you love, how you identify—all are welcome here. Our tagline is 'We're beer for you.' It is sincere when we [say] we know what it's like to feel like an outsider. We know what it's like to be blatantly discriminated against, and we will have none of that here."

As they were researching and visiting other breweries prior to their own opening, Loch and Pavlak found that many of the spaces reflected the owner's particular demographic or interests, which didn't always feel welcoming to them. "The owners of those spaces," Loch says, "they're building a place that they want to go to and that represents who they are. And that's how Urban Growler is [for us]." That is to say, Loch and Pavlak built a brewery where they, personally, would want to drink.

Urban Growler keeps its taproom at warmer temperatures than you might normally find in a taproom, in order to accommodate women's typically slower metabolisms. The owners also bought square-back chairs for the dining and bar areas that more easily allow purses to be hung off the back without falling off. Urban Growler offers a range of lower-alcohol beers as well as a variety of beer styles so groups can share and tell stories about what they are drinking. The brewery is embracing the trend of alternative beverages, both alcoholic and not.

The flight paddles at Urban Growler show off the brewery's distinctive logo.

Hard seltzer, kombucha, cream soda, lemonade, and hoppy water have all been on the Urban Growler menu. None of this is to say the brewery is "for women" any more than other breweries are "for men." All these details are simply by-products of Pavlak and Loch's desire to build a brewery that represents them.

"When we first opened, people were just amazed there was a woman brewer. They'd say, 'Come on, who's really brewing the beer?'" master brewer Deb Loch told the *Star Tribune* in 2018. "We don't get those questions anymore. To me, it's changing a little bit."

As Jerard Fagerberg wrote in *Thrillist* in 2017, "Luckily, Loch is becoming less of an anomaly in her community. In her two years in the commercial space, she's seen a determined uptick in the number of women joining her ranks. It's still not quite enough, but if her example can convince anyone that their gender isn't a factor, then that's her definition of success."

Loch told Fagerberg, "More and more women are realizing this is an option and that you don't have to have a beard to be a brewer. There's the scientific aspect of it, and there's the creative aspect of it, and both parts are gender neutral. You just have to trust that you can do it."

Other woman-identified brewers in Minnesota include Melissa Rainville of Summit Brewing, Lauren Miller of Indeed Brewing, Shannon Stroh of Surly Brewing, Jordan Nordby of Utepils Brewing in Minneapolis, Ariel Keeton at Badger Hill Brewing in Shakopee, Debbie Torgerson of Torg Brewery in Spring Lake Park, Lori Ertl of Under Pressure Brewing in Golden Valley, and Kathleen Culhane of Sidhe (now closed).

SOWING SUDS

While much of the 1,850 barrels Urban Growler brewed in 2018 went to cans of their flagship beers (Cowbell Cream Ale, Midwest IPA, and De-Lovely Porter), the brewers are still devoted to small-batch experimentation. In 2018, the brewery canned and distributed eight beers in addition to their flagships—placing new labels over their preprinted cans—and released even more in the taproom.

Urban Growler is still using the ten-barrel system it brewed with when the brewery opened. The relatively smaller system allows for creativity and flexibility with beers that may never (or, more likely, will never) see the market outside the taproom's historic walls. Loch isn't the type to get into a lazy routine or play it safe; her creativity and curiosity show through in the brewery's innovative styles and recipes.

Urban Growler's Plow to Pint series has been part of the brewery's lineup since the beginning, and it gets at exactly what Urban Growler is trying to achieve: connection and community. The beers have a local focus, using ingredients harvested locally, and they usually have a twist. The series brings together farmers, urban gardeners, the brewery team,

From the Plow to Pint series to the flagship Cowbell Cream Ale, Urban Growler beers offer something for everyone.

and consumers. Loch says the collaborative spirit references the Urban Growler logo: a circular shape similar to a farmer's plow that symbolizes the community being "all in this together." Beers in the series include a Belgian-style witbier brewed with blueberries harvested from the family-owned Highland Valley Farm, an apple and cranberry orchard saison, a wild rice brown ale, and a honey IPA.

BEERS TO KNOW

Cowbell Cream Ale: "A 'transitional beer' that may just lure the American light lager fans into the world of craft beer. Our cream ale is light gold in color and low in bitterness; the specialty malt and flaked maize add complexity to this smooth thirst quencher." 5.2% ABV, 20 IBU

De-Lovely Porter: "Smooth and dark yet refreshing. You don't have to wait until the snow falls to enjoy this dark beauty." 5.6% ABV, 33 IBU

Imperial Smoked Chipotle Porter: A seasonal specialty. "Big and malty with assertive chocolate flavors and undertones of caramel sweetness followed by a wave of chipotle heat and savory smoke." 8.2% ABV, 58 IBU

Kentucky Uncommon: "Previously known as City Day Ale. This is a Kentucky Common–style brew; this style was popular before Prohibition but disappeared as time went on. ... Kentucky Common takes the bourbon recipe and modifies it for beer. Instead of distilling the mash and making bourbon, we boil it and add hops—and our own twist of course." 5.5% ABV, 40 IBU

Midwest IPA: "An English-style IPA with a sturdy malt backbone that helps to balance the hop bitterness in this IPA." The blue-ribbon winner for IPAs at the 2012 Minnesota State Fair. 6.2% ABV, 60 IBU

A bright neon sign above the bar welcomes patrons to Bauhaus Brew Labs with a hearty cheer of *Gemütlichkeit!*

BAUHAUS BREW LABS

A FAMILY-OWNED BREWERY WITH A SENSE OF PLAY AND ADVENTURE

Minneapolis, Minnesota
Opened: July 2014
Barrels produced (2019): 9,635; 11th largest in state by production
The Team: Lydia Haines, owner and CEO
Matt Schwandt, owner, COO, and head brewer
Maura Hagerty Schwandt, owner and director of marketing, communications, and events
Drew Hurst, director of operations
Chris Squire, lead brewer

IT'S ALL IN THE ATTITUDE

Bauhaus Brew Labs is an anchor in the Northeast Minneapolis brewery scene. Its name comes from the German school of art of the same name, which bridged the gap between artistic beauty and utilitarian functionality to produce modern architecture, minimalist furniture, and household goods based on industrial forms. Rather than taking a minimalist, functionalist approach to the brewery, however, Bauhaus Brew Labs emphasizes punchy colors and aims to bring art into contact with daily life. The effect is an industrial taproom splashed with bold colors and even bolder parties. Head brewer Matt Schwandt hit it on the nose when he described the brewery's aesthetic to *The Growler* in 2014: "What we're going for is Monsters, Inc. meets Willy Wonka."

Bright murals, punchy artwork, and irreverent beer names create a party-like environment at the taproom, which was originally built as a foundry for the Crown Iron Works Company in 1905. Events like WWE-style wrestling, Skateboard Olympics, and vintage motorcycle shows fill the calendar. In March 2019, Bauhaus held a celebration of life ceremony—complete with eulogy—for a canned beer they retired.

Bauhaus's director of operations, Drew Hurst, attributes the brewery's innovative promotions and impressive parties to the team's creativity. Bauhaus also has a strong family orientation, with heavy representation on the brewery staff from the families of CEO Lydia Haines (mother Kathy, father Howard, and sister Leah) and of her husband, COO and head brewer Matt Schwandt (brothers Mike and Mark and sister-in-law Maura).

The staff is a collection of "musicians, scientists, and artists" who are committed to authenticity in everything they do. Hurst says, "There's a kind of X factor that is being genuine and being authentic." And, according to Hurst, Bauhaus worked hard to build this reputation. The team made choices to lean into the things they love and what resonates with their customers. As the events grew, so did customers' expectations. So the Bauhuas team won't throw "bogus events." For ideas that survive that litmus test, they must decide: *do we have what it takes to follow through?* "If not," says Hurst, "we probably shouldn't do it."

Authenticity at Bauhaus is not just about throwing parties, however. It's also about creating a welcoming atmosphere every day. A neon sign over the taproom bar bears the German word *Gemütlichkeit* (gih-moot-lih-kite). *Gemütlichkeit* lacks a direct English translation, but it's something akin to "cheers." Hurst says it is a toast to "all that's good in life: to friends, to family. It's like that feeling of warmth and welcome and acceptance that you get when you're doing things you like with people you like." Hurst says the term serves as a philosophical guideline for all the company does.

. . . AND IN THE BEER

Drew Hurst felt the warmth of *gemütlichkeit* on his very first visit to Bauhaus. One night after his band got done practicing at their nearby rehearsal space, he stopped by for a beer at the new neighborhood brewery. He was so enchanted by the Stargrazer schwarzbier that he flagged down the first person he saw in a Bauhaus shirt to praise the beer. That person was Matt Schwandt, the head brewer.

Hurst built a relationship with the people at the brewery, helping out busing tables when the taproom was busy and working special events. After a year, he joined the team full time and eventually became the director of operations. His connection to Bauhaus was organic and driven by the clear chemistry he had with the team there, as well as the welcoming environment.

The brewery's philosophy of approachability also extends to its beer list, characterized by a reliable set of approachable lagers with occasional ventures into more trendy styles. As Hurst explains, "It's very intentional that we don't [have] twelve hazy IPAs on tap or twelve barrel-aged something-or-others on tap. We do those things and we have fun with those things, but our flagship is a pilsner. In 2014 when we opened, no one else was doing a pilsner as a flagship; it was all IPAs. [We were] able to lean into that pretty hard and make beer styles that weren't predicated on [a patron] being a craft beer expert."

That's not to say head brewer Schwandt isn't an expert. His interest in craft beer began in the late 1990s when he was working at a

PARTY CITY

While Bauhaus has hosted dozens of events throughout the years, they have four major annual gatherings:

Pupper Bowl (1,500–2,000 human attendees): Hosted in February, this dog-focused event features all types of "bowl" games, with dogs divided by weight class. Needless to say, it's adorable.

Liquid Zoo (20,000–25,000 attendees): This May rager takes place during the annual Art-A-Whirl art crawl in Northeast Minneapolis. Killer local bands, great craft beer, and bites from local chefs bring all-day festivity. Whether you're a Bauhaus newbie or a years-long regular, you feel like an insider at this party.

Anniversary Party (5,000–7,000 attendees): Every July, Bauhaus throws down for a birthday party rife with specialty beers, talented musical acts, and great food.

Schwandtoberfest (5,000–7,000 attendees): This late-September Oktoberfest party pairs a Märzen beer release with the Schwandt family name. There are casked beers, steins aplenty, and—of course—live tunes.

Bauhaus packs in the fun at events like Liquid Zoo, held during Northeast Minneapolis's annual Art-A-Whirl. *Photo by Tim McGuire*

brewpub in Nashville. From there, he joined up with a homebrewers' society, where his appreciation for quality beer only deepened. As Schwandt told the *Pioneer Press* in 2014, "I … discovered that if you pay attention to your product, you can make some really good beer. From the get-go, I had this focus on improving and exploring new styles. Then I started crafting my own beers that weren't necessarily in any category but that I enjoyed. I drifted toward German styles, putting my own twist on them." That twist on German brews eventually transferred to both the name and the primary beer styles of the brewery Schwandt helped to found.

And, just as the German Bauhaus school of art brought design to the masses, Bauhaus Brew Labs is doing the same with beer. Part of that is making sure customers feel welcome. Hurst says, "I never want anyone to come in here and feel like they don't belong." The company is proud that its customer base covers a range of age, race, gender, and interest demographics.

Hurst adds, "If someone comes here and they've never had an IPA in their life, well, no worries: we've got plenty of other stuff to try. But if you are curious about an IPA, we're going to walk you through it and let you try a couple things, and we're not going to make you feel belittled or like you don't belong."

SELTZER BUBBLING UP

Several Minnesota breweries have tried their hand at producing hard seltzer. Hard seltzer is a simple alternative for non-beer drinkers in the taproom, and it diversifies the brewery's distributed offerings. Perhaps most importantly, it fulfills a growing consumer demand. Hard seltzer grew from 0.9 percent of the alcohol market in 2018 to 2.5 percent in 2019.

The Growler reported in December 2019 that Minnesota breweries were on to the hard seltzer trend: "Locally, hard seltzer exploded as a category in 2019. With only two local brands commercially available in the market at the end of 2018, by the end of 2019, Minnesota will have had 28 seltzers hit taps and packaged in cans."

Bauhaus joined the seltzer game in September 2019, when it announced a line of hard seltzers called BOLO. The team tested the beverage in the taproom in January of that year and perfected it before making the jump to a packaged product. The Brewers Association notes that hard seltzers typically follow the formula of market-leading brands like White Claw, and BOLO is no exception. Like White Claw, BOLO seltzers are made from fermented sugar (and are therefore gluten free) and ring in at about a hundred calories and five percent ABV.

BOLO seltzers are a distinct brand from Bauhaus in terms of both imagery and marketing tactics. Hurst says this is because Bauhaus "didn't want to cannibalize shelf space for craft beer." He recognizes the markets for craft beer and seltzer may cross over, but they don't overlap entirely by any means. So it was important for Bauhaus to build a standalone brand. Most importantly, the team didn't want to take themselves too seriously with this product.

Hurst says the irreverent attitude with the hard seltzer line is partly due to industry attitudes toward the product itself. Beer industry

The Bauhaus taproom is well known and easily recognized for its bright colors and murals.

vets may have made fun of the hard seltzer trend, but they were also the first to drink it at a party. It may be a trend, and even considered sacrilegious by beer purists, but hard seltzers can taste good, and they meet a need in the marketplace. So Bauhaus shrugged its shoulders and went for it. "Yes, it's kind of stupid," Hurst says. "And yes, it's okay."

BEERS TO KNOW

Wonderstuff Pilsner: "Wonderstuff delivers the clean, balanced flavors you'd expect from a Bohemian-style pilsner, but with a powerful, citrus hop twist." 5.1 % ABV, 30 IBU

Lounge Wizard Juicy Pale Ale: "Showcases juicy hop flavors and aromas reminiscent of pungent tropical fruit and candied citrus with a soft, pillowy texture and a pleasantly dry finish." 5.2% ABV, 40 IBU

Sky-Five! IPA: "Generous late hop additions provide loads of hop flavor, with just enough bitterness. Notes of citrus, passionfruit, and spice are supported by German and British malts, building a full-flavored yet balanced IPA." 6.4% ABV, 70 IBU

Stargrazer Black Lager: "This schwarzbier is a jet-black mystery, delivering a surprisingly light body and bright hop profile without the heavy roast qualities you find in most dark beers." 5% ABV, 28 IBU

Lounge Wizard, a juicy pale ale, took the place of the Wagon Party lager in the brewery's core lineup while staying true to the Bauhaus philosophy of making beer that's approachable.

AWARDS TO KNOW

Bauhaus is a two-time winner of "Best Taproom" by *City Pages* (2017 and 2019).

2016 World Beer Cup: Wonderstuff, Bronze Medal, International-Style Lager category

2017 World Beer Awards: Stargrazer, USA Winner, German-Style Schwarzbier

2017 World Beer Awards: Wagon Party, USA Winner, West Coast Style Lager

2017 World Beer Awards: Wonderstuff, USA Gold Medal

2018 *The Growler* "Kind-of-a-Big-Deal" Award: Wonderstuff, Best Lager

2018 World Beer Awards: Hairbanger, USA Silver Medal

2018 World Beer Awards: Wonderstuff, USA Gold Medal

2019 Brewers Cup Awards: Stargrazer, Third Place, Amber & Dark Lagers

FINNEGANS BREW CO.

THE FIRST BREWERY IN THE WORLD TO DONATE 100 PERCENT OF ITS PROFITS TO CHARITY

Minneapolis, Minnesota
Company founded: September 2000
Taproom opened: March 2018
Barrels produced (2019): 3,264; 23rd largest in state by production
The Team: Jacquie Berglund, cofounder and CEO

BREWING FOR GOOD

Jacquie Berglund has a gift for bringing together good business and good deeds. Finnegans Brew Co. is the result of that gift.

Berglund's light bulb came in two parts: She was first inspired by her boss, Kieran Folliard, when she was working at the Local restaurant in downtown Minneapolis. When talking with a friend about her job—which was basically selling beer all day—the friend told her Kieran was such a local celebrity that "he could have his own beer and put his mug on it like Paul Newman." Newman, an actor, director, and race car driver, created a salad dressing brand called Newman's Own. He donated all profits to charity, totaling well over $500 million after his company brought out dozens of new product lines.

Then, Berglund heard an interview with Billy Shore, the executive director of Share Our Strength, a nonprofit organization that aims to end childhood hunger. Shore supported his nonprofit through a for-profit consulting business, and that's where Berglund had her real aha moment. She recalls, "It was like my hair was on fire. I'm like, that is the coolest thing ever. I want to do that."

She approached Kieran with the idea to brew their own "craft beer with a mission" for the pub. Berglund would support her own future nonprofit—which would be the Finnegans Community Fund—with the beer she and Kieran produced and sold. Rather than competing for grants or soliciting donations, Berglund wanted to support good work with a beer business. With no brewing experience of her own, Berglund was running on pure hair-on-fire energy. "I had no background in the beer industry," she recalls. "I did no market research. It was a hundred percent passion."

At first, the beer was named after Folliard: Kieran's Irish Ale. Folliard sold the recipe to Berglund for a dollar in 2000, thus transferring the rights from his restaurant group to her beer company. They renamed the beer Finnegans after brainstorming names at the bar at the Local restaurant. Berglund and Folliard would order beers by different names to a hypothetical bartender to test out how it felt and sounded to order the beer. When Folliard said "give me a Finnegans," Jacquie knew that was it.

Since its inception, Finnegans contract brewed the beer with local regional brewers. It started with James Page Brewing, formerly in Northeast Minneapolis, and moved to Summit Brewing in 2003. The operation remained at Summit for over a dozen years, with the Summit team brewing and packaging Berglund's recipe.

By opting for a contract brewing arrangement, Berglund didn't have to learn how to brew or hire a brewer, and she didn't have to invest in the massive overhead of equipment, space, and ingredients. Plus, "I never have to worry about quality," she told the *Pioneer Press* in a 2014 interview. Because the beer was brewed by contract, Berglund was the sole employee of Finnegans for nine years, and the rest of the work at the company was completed by volunteers.

Finnegans is truly one of a kind in the beer world. Its 100-percent donation model is the second-longest running of its type, following the Newman's Own Foundation. Finnegans will hit $2 million in donations in 2020, an amazing feat for any company, especially one that had only one employee for half its existence. To make the model scalable, Finnegans partners with local food banks in each state where it distributes the beer. The food banks use the money to purchase produce from local, organic growers at a dollar per pound. That produce is then donated to local food shelves. In Minnesota, the process is done locally, so beer sold in Duluth, for example, supports Duluth farmers. Berglund gets excited as she outlines this process: "I'm super passionate about a sustainable business model that you can do well and do good."

Jacquie Berglund was inspired to bring together her passions for good beer and doing good when she opened Finnegans Brew Co.

OUT OF THE NEST

Minnesota's craft beer scene changed drastically in 2011 with the passage of the taproom bill. Berglund noticed the uptick in competition, and she saw how breweries were achieving great profit margins in their own taprooms. If she wanted to compete, she knew she would have to open a taproom.

In 2018, Finnegans opened its own facility in the Elliot Park neighborhood of downtown Minneapolis. The building is home to a brewery, a two-story taproom and event space, and a social innovation incubator/coworking space called FINNOVATION Lab. A 4,000-square-foot patio leaves plenty of room for community gatherings of all types.

Berglund chose the space intentionally: it is two blocks from the old Finnegans business offices and four blocks from her studio apartment. The Elliot Park neighborhood is also "complicated," says Berglund. It has the highest poverty rate in downtown Minneapolis, yet four blocks away is the "most historically expensive development project ever in the history of Minnesota"—the billion-dollar-plus U.S. Bank Stadium. For Berglund, opening her brewery in the Elliot Park neighborhood was a matter of walking the talk of Finnegans. She says, "It really seemed like this neighborhood needed a place to create more community, a social place to hang out, a place to come together."

In trying to foster a community-oriented space, the Finnegans taproom doesn't feel like a traditional Minnesota taproom. Berglund, as always, wanted to do things differently. She designed Finnegans as an "un-taproom." The seating options all have backs so you can settle in comfortably, the acoustics allow for easy conversation, and coziness is key. Berglund brought in an agency to help select the woods, fabrics, and textures of the space. Local artisans created the bar and wood carvings from Minnesota basswood.

While the beer sold in the taproom was brewed on-site, all of Finnegans's packaged beer was produced at Badger Hill's facility in Shakopee through an alternating proprietorship, or alt-prop, arrangement. In this setup, Finnegans's own brewers drove the twenty

The Finnegans taproom is dark and comfortable, inviting guests to stay a while—not unlike an Irish pub.

miles south to brew and package the beer themselves, rather than having the host brewery do that work in Finnegans's name, as is the case for contract brewing. In 2020, Finnegans moved all of their brewing downtown to bring that process in-house to make the work a little simpler and more efficient.

FINNOVATION AND PHILANTHROPY

In addition to supporting the Finnegans Community Fund through beer sales, Berglund also practices philanthropy through her reverse food truck as well as the FINNOVATION Lab.

Rather than serving food, the Finnegans food truck takes food donations. In partnership with the Food Group, the Reverse Food Truck accepts food and monetary donations to help further Finnegans's mission of ending hunger. Volunteers drive the truck to beer festivals, community events, and anyplace else it is requested.

FINNOVATION Lab, launched by Berglund in May 2018, is a social business catalyst that provides resources, workshops, fellowships, grants, and 13,000 square feet of coworking space to community-minded entrepreneurs and upstarts. "I think the more social entrepreneurs we have," Berglund says, "the healthier communities we're going to have. Businesses that care about doing well and doing good have a sustainable model. They're passionate about making a difference in the community. And my whole thing is just to make the world a better place."

BEERS TO KNOW

Finnegans Irish Amber: The first beer developed by Finnegans, along with James Page Brewing, and the brewery's only beer for twelve years. "We made the Irish ale to be like a gateway beer," Berglund explains, "so light beer drinkers could dabble in this pond here and enjoy it. It's not too hoppy, not too malty—really middle of the road, medium flavor and body." The website describes it as "a full-flavored, medium-bodied ale with a caramelly, malty finish." 4.75% ABV, 20 IBU

Dead Irish Poet Extra Stout: Developed in 2014 as the brewery's third beer, this stout was created with the assistance of Damian McConn, legendary Irish brewer for Summit. It is named in homage to Irish writers such as James Joyce, author of *Finnegans Wake*. "This unique Cork-style stout has a smooth roasted quality with dark chocolate and stone fruit notes." Dead Irish Poet is a winter seasonal offering. 7% ABV, 38 IBU

AWARDS TO KNOW

Finnegans and owner Jacquie Berglund have received many awards in recognition of their entrepreneurship, business model, and philanthropy.

LUPULIN BREWING COMPANY

FROM THE STRIP MALL TO THE BIG LEAGUES

Big Lake, Minnesota
Opened: April 2015
Barrels produced (2019): 6,160; 13th largest in state by production
The Team: Jeff Zierdt, cofounder, president, and CEO
Matt Schiller, vice president of operations
Ben Haugen, head production brewer
Aaron Zierdt, head innovation brewer (small batch)

STRIP MALL BEGINNINGS

To study Lupulin Brewing is to understand the growth potential in the craft beer industry. Located in one of the Twin Cities metro area's many innocuous exurb strip malls but distributing to countless retailers across the state and beyond, Lupulin has a story that combines great beer and great business.

Garage homebrew buddies Jeff Zierdt and Matt Schiller opened Lupulin Brewing in April 2015. Each kept his respective full-time job and expected to keep it for several years to come. Jeff's son Aaron joined the team as a brewer at the ten-barrel brewhouse, which was informally separated from the taproom by just a bench. It was in that 3,000-square-foot space that Lupulin built its brand, producing in its first eight months a humble 330 barrels, featuring a chocolate porter, a Belgian blonde, and the Resin Rapture IPA. That was just the beginning. In every year since, the brewery has blown the team's business projections clear out of the water. Lupulin doubled its barrel production each year, making it one of the fastest growing breweries in the country.

Luckily for Lupulin, the strip mall brewery backed up to a 15,000-square-foot warehouse, allowing for the opportunity to expand. Only six months in, Lupulin's owners doubled their footprint so they could triple their cooler space and add twenty barrels for aging the beer. The expansion allowed them to brew and store a wider variety of beers and increase the number of tap lines at the taproom. At first, rather than investing the necessary money and space for a canning line, Lupulin worked with NorthStar Mobile Canning while the team focused on the brewing.

That spring, the two cofounders and the brewer kicked into the next gear of entrepreneurialism after attending the 2016 Craft Brewers Conference in Philadelphia. While they were in that neck of the woods, the trio traveled around, drinking and researching New England–style IPAs and hazy IPAs. When they tasted the haze, they saw their futures. Upon the team's return to Big Lake, the hazy double IPA they titled Blissful Ignorance was born, and it launched Lupulin into orbit. As Jeff Zierdt explains, "We released [Blissful Ignorance] in August of 2016 in bottles and on tap, and it was gone in less than a week." Expanding the brewery and production system was necessary, and it needed to happen fast.

Following the smashing success of the Blissful Ignorance release, Zierdt and Schiller quickly arranged an investor meeting in the hopes of securing additional capital for an expansion. They told the investors, who comprised 10 percent of the business ownership, that they were willing to give up 20 percent of their shares for a bank loan, and they told the investors how much was available and how much they needed for the expansion. Within five minutes of making their proposal, Zierdt and Schiller had checks in hand. Now it was time to get down to (even more) work.

They expanded the brewing operations into the available warehouse space behind the brewery and erected a formal wall between the taproom and brewhouse so they could brew, keg, and can all day long without disrupting taproom patrons. Production capacity increased massively as they installed four thirty-barrel fermenters and a thirty-barrel brite tank in January 2017. Co-owner and brewer Schiller quit his day job and began working for Lupulin full time.

From there, the brewery's rapid growth was built in large part on distribution (as opposed to taproom sales), and it all began with Blissful Ignorance, the first beer they brewed on the expanded system.

HOOEY
ORDER HERE

In February 2017, Blissful Ignorance hit the market in cans. "It blew off the shelves," Zierdt recalls proudly. "We couldn't keep up. We went from a list of half a dozen liquor stores to a waiting list of more than a hundred overnight." Soon, Schiller and co-brewer Aaron Zierdt were working from three in the morning until ten at night to brew three turns a day of the popular hazy beer.

EXPLOSIVE EXPANSION

As the success of Blissful Ignorance continued, Jeff Zierdt noticed that their Batch 100, the hazy IPA that would later become Hooey, was also performing well in the market. The IPA was put on tap at Republic, a popular Minneapolis craft beer bar. It soon became the number-one seller among fifty other greats at the bar.

Republic was "where Hooey made its mark," Zierdt says. "That's what got us into *Thrillist* magazine." The beer was named one of the best IPAs in America by the popular food and drink magazine for two years running. It was clear to Lupulin's owners that they needed to package Hooey as well and leverage it for the business's continued growth.

It was around this time, in the spring of 2017—Lupulin's second anniversary—that Jeff Zierdt came on full time, three years ahead of their business projections: "My first objective was asking, 'How do we continue the growth? What do we need to do next?'" In his prior career, Zierdt had managed $300 million businesses and had overseen expansions several times larger and more expensive than Lupulin's. He had been around the block when it came to managing growth, and he was ready to put his expertise to full use at the brewery.

The Lupulin Brewing taproom in Big Lake attracts locals and cabin-bound travelers alike.

The next vital step in the business plan was to secure the space and bring more control over the operation. "So," Zierdt explains, "we entered negotiations with the landlord to buy the entire 22,500 square feet—the building that we're in now. We closed on that deal in October 2017. It took five months to negotiate. It wasn't fun, but we needed to negotiate because we had a canning line on the way."

At the time, Lupulin was releasing their Apricot Blonde and Hooey cans almost back to back. "That pretty much put us to our knees in terms of what our capacity was," says Zierdt. To keep up with production demand that fall, Lupulin was able to hire a highly qualified brewer who came with both commercial experience and a chemistry degree: Ben Haugen from Third Street Brewhouse in Cold Spring.

In late 2017 and early 2018, the team added two sixty-barrel fermenters and a sixty-barrel brite tank, hired another full-time brewer, increased its sales force, hired more delivery drivers, and purchased new delivery vans.

Then, in June of 2018, Lupulin closed on a $4 million expansion deal that allowed it to purchase a semi-automated thirty-barrel brewing system for installation in 2019 as well as upgrade the canning line from thirty-five to eighty cans per minute, a growth rate that aligned with the tripling of the brewing system.

Lupulin brought on its first distribution partners in January 2019; the brewery had been self-distributing up to that point. The new thirty-barrel brewing system was up and running in February 2019, and four more sixty-barrel fermenters were installed in April followed by three more sixty-barrel fermenters in June to meet the demand of additional distribution contracts.

In 2018, Zierdt projected that Lupulin would produce 6,500 barrels of beer. About 6,000 of those barrels go out the back door into the market—70–80 percent as cans; the remainder as kegs. The current brewhouse has a capacity of 8,500 barrels, which means Lupulin is operating at about 76 percent of capacity. "You never want to run everything at 100 percent," Zierdt says. "I mean, that's how we

The popularity of Hooey hazy IPA helped spur rapid expansion for Lupulin's distribution plans.

had been running, so 80 percent is a good number." Their reported production was 6,160 barrels, just shy of the projection: "It's been just constant expansion to get to where we are today, and we're still expanding."

IPAS—AND MORE

Lupulin's business was built on IPAs, and Zierdt believes the style isn't going away any time soon. But that doesn't mean the Lupulin team is holding back in other categories.

In April 2019, Lupulin revealed its plans to venture into sours and unveiled a new brand, Scribbled Lines, which the brewery described as a "creative exploration into the world of sour beer. Our focus is on traditional, old world methods, with some modern twists." It was an idea they had been developing for a while; barrels that are now part of the Scribbled Lines program have been accumulating in Lupulin's warehouse since 2016. Because the brewery was known mostly for its IPAs, it decided to create a new brand and identity for its sours. As the

A BREWERY HERO

For a brewery that grew at the rate and scale that Lupulin did, Minnesota's legal restrictions on breweries had a profound effect on its long-term plans, far beyond simply limiting growler sales. For Jeff Zierdt, it meant he was limited in what he could do to support a cause that was deeply important and personal to him.

In November 2018, Lupulin Brewing and Mankato Brewery released a collaboration hazy IPA called Hero. The beer honored Jonathan Zierdt, Jeff Zierdt's brother and a friend of Mankato Brewery owner Tim Tupy. Jonathan battled prostate cancer for years. With a label depicting Jonathan as a cartoon superhero, the collaboration beer raised money to benefit the Jonathan Zierdt Cancer Fund and, later, the Box Love

Lupulin seemingly is always adding new tanks to its brewhouse in order to keep up with production demands.

Campaign, which puts together boxes of items to support and comfort cancer patients as well as resources for patients, families, and caregivers.

Because Hero IPA was brewed at Mankato Brewery's facility, however, Jeff was not allowed to sell the beer at his own brewery; by law, Minnesota brewers can sell only alcoholic beverages that are brewed on-site. This legal restraint prevented Zierdt from selling the beer himself to raise money for his own brother's cancer fund. Jonathan Zierdt passed away in March 2019. The next batch of Hero IPA was brewed at Lupulin Brewing so Jeff could put it on tap.

brewery explained to *The Growler*, "In order to better tell the story of what we are doing with our sour barrel program, we found it was better to just have a whole different label."

Meanwhile, Lupulin is broadening its IPA offerings as well, and Zierdt says it is "caught up in" the hazy Northeast/New England IPA craze. More than just a trend, the hazy IPA is here to stay, as evidenced by the national Brewers Association adding it as an official style in its 2018 guidelines. The style is characterized by straw to deep gold colors with any range of cloudiness. Juicy/hazy IPAs are minimally malty and packed with hop aroma and flavors. Despite the major role hops play in these beers, they typically have a low perceived bitterness. Fruity esters from fermentation may contribute to a sense of sweetness and complement the hop profile. Some hazy IPAs earn the title of "juicy" when large, late additions of hops are included in the recipe.

The staggering successes of the IPAs Blissful Ignorance and Hooey put Lupulin on the map, so it only made sense for the brewery to cash in on its IPA-centric brand with a beer festival dedicated to the style. Zierdt had noticed other breweries hosting niche festivals, such as Fair State's Mixed Culture or Junkyard's Rare Beer Picnic. He saw that a festival could provide the opportunity for a brewery like Lupulin to solidify its presence within a style category, like IPAs.

So Lupulin launched the IPA Invitational in the summer of 2018. Twenty-three breweries attended the inaugural festival with the best of their best IPAs.

The 2019 IPA Invitational featured twenty-seven breweries, half Minnesotan and half out-of-staters who could introduce their beers to Minnesota's hop-loving population. Lupulin requires that a brewer or owner pour their own beer at the festival. This requirement grants beer geeks direct access to the source of their favorite hop-forward flavors. Lupulin plans to scale the festival to include up to fifty breweries while still keeping the experience intimate by capping ticket sales.

Zierdt predicts that the future of IPAs may include experimentations in yeast and fermentation, which could allow beer to be packaged as much as two weeks faster than previously possible with traditional yeasts. The potential for new flavors is just as important as the ability to maximize brewhouse efficiency and get cans in hands. But really, all we need to know is Zierdt is sure the style isn't going anywhere.

CROSSING THE BORDER

If you have been following along this far, you know by now that Lupulin Brewing does not think small. Beyond buying new equipment and launching new brands, Lupulin took the major step of opening a second taproom.

In June 2019, Lupulin announced its acquisition of Hydra Beer Company in Sioux Falls, South Dakota. Expanding to a second location within Minnesota was the brewery's first choice, but it wasn't an option. "We'd love to have another taproom in Minnesota," Matt Schiller told the Sioux Falls *Argus Leader*, "but the state law won't allow it. It's really stupid."

Still, opening a taproom in Sioux Falls does have its benefits. First, the city is one of the fastest growing metro areas in the nation. Additionally, it's simply easier to run a beer business there. Zierdt comments, "In Minnesota, you almost need an attorney to read through all of the statutes and the requirements in terms of the liquor

Carefully labeled barrels are nestled against a back wall of the Lupulin brewhouse, aging a range of beers within.

laws and everything." But in South Dakota, Zierdt says, laws are far friendlier to breweries.

Reporting on Lupulin's acquisition of Hydra, *The Growler* noted that opening multiple taproom locations was likely a strategy that more breweries would pursue, as the smaller, taproom-based breweries were enjoying greater growth compared to larger distributing breweries. In a haze of popularity and growth, Lupulin is accomplishing both: it achieved massive distribution while investing in quality drinking experiences at a pair of mini-destination taprooms. The Big Lake location, despite being in a strip mall off the highway, is a comfortable place to drink a couple craft beers. Quirky touches like sinks made out of bisected kegs remind patrons that no matter how much the brewery might grow, it was started by a couple of guys who just really loved craft beer. Only time will tell how else they might grow.

Hooey is opaque and hazy with yeast and hop oils, which are not filtered out from the brew.

BEERS TO KNOW

Blissful Ignorance Double IPA: "Inspired by the wonderful hoppy beers coming out of the Northeast. This Double IPA is loaded with waves of some of the juiciest hops available. Citra, Mosaic, and Columbus blend together to make this hop juice. Intentionally left hazy with yeast in suspension to create a soft mouthfeel and enhance the flavor of this wonderfully hoppy beer." 9% ABV, 70 IBU

CPB Chocolate Peanut Butter Porter: "Layers of decadent chocolate and peanut butter built into a rich oatmeal porter make this beer impossible to have just one. We're not sorry." 5.25% ABV, 20 IBU

Fashion Mullet: "Business in the front, party in the rear. This hop bomb is one part East Coast haze-bro (Citra), and one part old-school West Coast (Simcoe). Don't pick a side in this fight—you won't win." 6.5% ABV, 60 IBU

Hooey Hazy IPA: "This IPA is hopped with a ridiculous amount of the juiciest hops available. In order to bring you the most hop flavor possible, we intentionally leave yeast and hop oils in the beer by not filtering them out." 6.2% ABV, 60 IBU

Javatized Coffee Stout: "We Javatized this stout with freshly roasted coffee from our friends at Paradise Coffee Roasters. With flavors of fresh coffee, dark cocoa, and a balanced sweetness, it's perfect for any time of day." 6% ABV, 20 IBU

Sophistry: "An IPA series that we created after installing our new, state-of-the-art brewhouse in order to explore new hops and hopping techniques. Each iteration of this series is an exploration into creating new flavors and techniques in crafting IPA. Expect big and unique flavors with each new release."

AWARDS TO KNOW

Lupulin has been honored with several local awards for best brewery and beverage in the nearby towns of Monticello and Elk River, and *City Pages* named it "Best Suburban Brewery" in 2018. The brewery has also received numerous awards for its beers from state and national sources.

2015 Autumn Brew Review: Tropical Orgasm, Best Chocolate Porter

2017 Great American Beer Festival: Dortmunder, Gold Medal, Dortmunder or German-Style Oktoberfest category

2018 *The Growler* "Kind-of-a-Big-Deal" Award: Blissful Ignorance, Gold Medal, Double or Imperial IPA

2018 *The Growler* "Kind-of-a-Big-Deal" Award: Hooey, Silver Medal, Hazy or New England IPA

2018: *Thrillist*: Hooey, One of the 33 Best IPAs in the US

2019 Brewers Cup Awards: Blissful Ignorance, First Place, American Double IPAs

2019 Brewers Cup Awards: Night Witch, Third Place, Non-Sour Barrel-Aged Beers

2019 Brewers Cup Awards: Straight Hash Homie, Third Place, American Double IPAs

FORAGER BREWERY

A LITTLE BREWPUB WITH A BIG HEART FOR CRAFT

Rochester, Minnesota
Opened: August 2015
Barrels produced (2019): 757; 65th largest in state by production
The Team: Annie Henderson, owner
Austin Jevne, head brewer and co-owner

FORAGING FOR COMMUNITY

In early 2015, I was a senior in college and working as an intern at the coworking center where the folks from Forager Brewery in Rochester were working with a branding and marketing team to build their new brewpub. (I would later get a job with that marketing team.) At the coworking center, I got a firsthand look at the tenacity and resourcefulness of entrepreneur Annie Henderson and the ingenuity of brewer Austin Jevne. They were building a brewpub with the community in the forefront of their minds. They incorporated a rotating gallery within the brewpub, set up a coffee shop in the adjacent space, and hosted a local indoor marketplace. It was a treat to witness the vision of a community gathering place come together, from the sourcing of the décor to considering the different functionality of the building's spaces to creating a seasonal menu that aligned with local farmers.

Jevne had tried to start his own brewery several times before he finally succeeded with Forager. His first attempt was a St. Paul location where the financing fell through; then it was a restaurant he hoped to convert to a brewpub. Finally, he helped open the Thirsty Belgian in Rochester, a pub with a heavy focus on Belgian beer. At this point, Jevne was homebrewing while teaching servers at the pub how to pair Belgian beers with food. When one of the Thirsty Belgian owners encouraged Jevne to open his own brewery, he admitted that he had already thrown in the towel on that idea. That's when a friend told him, "I gotta introduce you to this woman who really gets stuff done."

Co-owner and head brewer Austin Jevne maintains a positive, curious attitude while running the Forager Brewery.

That woman was Annie Henderson, a Rochester entrepreneur, philanthropist, and local art advocate. And it is very accurate to say she gets stuff done.

Whenever a brewery announces its projected opening date, I usually add about six months to allow for unforeseen hiccups and delays in plans, and I'm usually right. Henderson, however, got Forager Brewery in Rochester up and running in about eight months flat. It seems her dauntlessness was exactly what Jevne needed to finally get it done and open a brewery.

Jevne says that a major factor in Forager's success, after about five years in operation, is that Henderson encourages the staff to be themselves. "The best aspect of being part of Forager is that creative freedom is never extinguished," says Jevne as he reflects on the variety of styles he has brewed over the course of some nine hundred batches. That creativity is evident in the diversity of his releases: barrel-aged milk stouts, push pop–style fruited sours, and a host of funky Belgian ales, to name a few.

Jevne says Forager also allowed him to bring together his other passions and experiences. His career prior to working in beer and restaurants included years at the Wedge Community Co-op in

Forager's glorious taproom is furnished with many foraged finds, from the bar top to the barnwood on the walls.

Minneapolis, where he learned about local farmers and food, and at the Minnesota Department of Natural Resources, where he gained a love for the outdoors and learned how to forage for ingredients. The brewpub got its name because much of the work involved foraging, whether for local ingredients to use in brewing or for materials to build the taproom (the space features reclaimed barnwood walls, repurposed apple crates for shelving, a salvaged bar top, and handmade penny tables, among other items).

Building on Jevne's values of emphasizing community and supporting farmers, Jevne and Henderson followed the less typical path of opening a brewpub as the venue to show off his creative brews. Since the taproom bill passed in 2011, only ten other brewpubs have opened in Minnesota. The other 160-plus breweries that got started during this time opted to function as brewery taprooms, and only a small number of those chose to include a kitchen in their operation. The more intimate brewpub model allowed Forager to stay community oriented and to operate at a scale where the team could buy directly from local farmers for their scratch menu.

Jevne reflects, "When we first started, there was the concept of potentially doing a distribution brewing company, but we wanted to be focused on a localized community center in our facility that was for everyone, not just for people who liked beer. … We wanted to be able to have a place for kids and adults, for book clubs—whatever they want to do here. And we felt that doing a distribution brewery wasn't going to open that same door."

HUMBLE BEGINNINGS TO HUMBLE FORAGER

Parts of Forager's business have changed over the years—the house coffee shop is now a café incubator, and the local market area has shrunk to make room for more beer barrels and additional restaurant seating—but a few key things stayed the same, including a commitment to making quality craft beer and food, collaborating with local farmers and artists, and never settling for what is easy, comfortable, or status quo.

By establishing the business as a brewpub, Jevne and Henderson had forfeited the ability to distribute Forager's beer beyond crowler and bottle sales out of the Rochester location. When Jevne's brews started to build a buzz among beer geeks outside of Minnesota, however, they realized they needed to come up with a new strategy that would allow them to showcase his beer-making skills to the wider world. So, in 2019, Forager announced plans to create a sister brand to the brewpub line. Named Humble Forager, the distribution-only brand is contract brewed by Octopi Brewing in Waunakee, Wisconsin. The facility brews for the likes of Untitled Art, Mikerphone Brewing, and Horus Aged Ales.

As a purveyor of craft, Jevne is naturally protective of the beer list he's built, and Octopi met his standards for quality. "Their brew staff is phenomenal," he says. "They've got people from really, really great, successful breweries who have left to work at Octopi to get more experience brewing styles of beer that they didn't get to do at their previous breweries." Jevne worked with the team to scale his recipes and make the necessary tweaks to his process to maintain the integrity of his brews.

Forager had to alter the name for the new brewery due to distribution trademarks, but the modification is perfectly appropriate. They chose the adjective "humble" because that's exactly how Henderson and Jevne feel. They are humbled by consumer demand for their beer. When they opened their original brewery, they planned to make an impact in the Rochester community, but they never expected people from around the Midwest to come for their beer.

Henderson and Jevne know that with the distribution label they are entering a vastly different market than they've known with Forager the brewpub. In distribution, the brand is competing on store shelves and bar menus with dozens of other breweries, many of which might be more established. To help the brand stand out, they worked with a local artist to build a visual identity that aligned with Forager's mission, and they partnered with a distributor to drop limited quantities of beer into highly receptive craft beer markets in Minnesota, Wisconsin, Georgia, Florida, and Michigan. They'll partner only with draft accounts that respect the craft industry—those who clean their lines regularly and build well-rounded beer lists. Even in distribution, the brand's integrity will always stay central.

BEERS TO KNOW

Jevne's goal with Forager is to make approachable beers with strong flavors and a high shareability factor. He uses produce from local farms and pairs his brews with the kitchen's scratch menu. The brewpub offers an ever-rotating list of options.

Barrel-aged stouts: Jevne started brewing stouts as soon as Forager opened so he could have time to barrel age them for longer than most breweries do. While they're expensive to brew, and there's plenty of money sitting in the oak and adjuncts, the barrel-aged stouts are reputation builders for Forager. Jevne is always filling nooks and crannies of the brewery with more barrels. "That's where Annie and I butt heads," Jevne notes. "I say, 'I need more barrels.' And she's like, 'You can't have the room.' And I'm like, 'Okay, I'm going to sneak a barrel in there overnight.'"

Wild ales: Jevne says that other beers Forager started brewing right off the bat were Minnesota wild ales, spontaneously fermented beers, and mixed-culture beers. Brews in this vein incorporate "wild" yeast and other uncontrolled microflora rather than the typical store-bought yeast most brewers use. "I had some experiences when I was with the DNR foraging fruits and inoculating the beers with the yeast and bacteria that grew on the skins of those fruits. We were able to keep that culture alive and utilize it at Forager."

Fruited kettle sours: Brewing fruited kettle sours in the earliest days of the brewpub allowed Jevne to get these tart beers made with local fruit on tap right away. "And that's another huge piece of the distribution market," he adds, "these heavily fruited tart ales that I think bridge people from wine or cocktails into beer."

A blend of the Daydreaming saison. Forager's beer menu is designed to pair with its food menu, much like one might pair food with wine.

AWARDS TO KNOW

Forager was named 2016's best new brewery in Minnesota by RateBeer.

2017 Northern Lights Rare Beer Fest: Nillerzzzzz Imperial Stout, People's Choice Award

2018 Northern Lights Rare Beer Fest: Nillerzzzzz Imperial Stout, People's Choice Award

2019 Festival of Wood and Barrel-Aged Beer: Dollar Menu Pie Saison, Silver Medal

2019 RateBeer: Nillerzzzzz Imperial Stout, Best Beer in Minnesota

STEEL TOE BREWING

A BREWERY WITH BIG DREAMS OF STAYING SMALL

St. Louis Park, Minnesota
Brewery opened: August 2011
Taproom opened: February 2013
Barrels produced (2019): 3,791; 21st largest in state by production
The Team: Jason Schoneman, owner and brewer
Michael Wagner, head brewer and production manager

FROM WELDING TO WORT

When Jason Schoneman first started planning his own brewery, he and his wife, Hannah, asked themselves: *When is enough enough? How big would the brewery become?* When they opened Steel Toe Brewing in 2011, state law helped make that decision for them. Breweries were capped at 3,500 barrels if they wanted to sell growlers, and adding a taproom to the brewery wasn't an option at the time. That volume seemed manageable to them.

By avoiding taking on outside investors, Schoneman alleviated any external pressure to increase sales and improve return on investment at Steel Toe. He was able to focus on his dream without chasing the next big, moneymaking thing. It was about the craft more than the profits. "We never thought we'd get super wealthy owning a brewery," Schoneman says. All he wanted was to make great beer, save enough money to buy a house and start a family, and stop working for someone else.

Schoneman got started in beer—specifically, beer drinking—"a little too young," he admits. But his journey toward a life in craft beer took a winding road that prepared him well for his ultimate role as a brewery owner. Right out of high school, he got a job as a welder building Winnebagos. The Iowa native then went to school for toolmaking and eventually moved out to Colorado. "That's really where I saw that there was [craft] beer other than what was available in Iowa at the time, which was like Pete's Wicked Ale and Guinness," Schoneman reflects.

Head brewer Michael Wagner (left) and owner Jason Schoneman (right) have built Steel Toe into a premier Minnesota craft brewery.

Schoneman began his own homebrewing adventures in the nineties, and in 2000 he followed his girlfriend (now wife) Hannah out to Montana. He got a job at Lightning Boy Brewery in Belgrade as a cellarman—a job that usually involves a lot of cleaning, packaging, and equipment managing—and later became an assistant brewer.

Next he headed off for three months to the diploma course at the World Brewing Academy in Chicago and Munich. After completing the course, he got a job at Pelican Brewing in Oregon as a cellarman and worked his way up to head brewer over the course of four years.

Jason and Hannah Schoneman moved back to the Midwest in 2009 and started to work on launching a brewery of their own. Steel Toe Brewing opened in the Twin Cities suburb of St. Louis Park less than two years later.

While Schoneman shares a homebrewing origin story with many other craft brewers, his varied experience at commercial-scale breweries shows through in his brewery. Steel Toe beer is an industry favorite—and for a good reason.

Steel Toe has always stressed education and experience for its staff in order to ensure quality and efficiency in the brewhouse.

To help build the team, Schoneman brought on local industry professional Michael Wagner as a brewer in 2015. Wagner first got into craft brewing after a trip to Belgium and Germany inspired a beer awakening within him. He started homebrewing in the early 2000s and knew right away that he wanted to turn this passion into a career. Wagner recalls, "My girlfriend at the time, who's now my wife, had a good, stable job, and she said, 'Go do what you gotta do.'"

Wagner got a job as a beer buyer for Trader Joe's. Then, when Four Firkins—a specialty craft beer store—opened in St. Louis Park, Wagner landed a job there. "Through that experience I learned about the breadth and really the width of how far beer goes—the history and origins of it," Wagner says. "I just studied relentlessly on style origins, countries of origin, what makes saison so beautiful, and what makes German pilsner so great." In addition to his own self-directed studies, Wagner went through the Beer Judge Certification and Cicerone Certification Programs, both highly respected within the industry, and took the year-long diploma course in brewing science, fermentation science, and engineering at the American Brewers Guild.

EDUCATION FOR THE TRADE

Schoneman says he first came to his decision to open a brewery when he was working at Lightning Boy. He asked himself, *What are the steps we need to put in place to make sure we have the best chance of success?* He says that, at the time, in 2010, "there was no guarantee, and there still isn't a guarantee, that it's going to work. Education and experience, for most skilled trades, [that's what] you need in order to be successful."

While no entrepreneur would launch a business without doing their research first, Schoneman dedicated ten years to honing his craft, observing how breweries are run, gaining an education, and building his plan. "I saw it from the beginning as a career, as a profession, and as a trade that I wanted to master," he recalls. "And what happens when we get into this huge growth phase of the craft brewing industry is people see it as an investment." Schoneman says that this massive industry growth has changed the way breweries are started: rich uncles provide funding for garage brewers who have little to no brewing education and no business savvy.

Wagner agrees, "There's all these things that come into play on this scale that you just can't learn homebrewing. You can learn on the fly, and some people can do that. You can also fail really easily that way. You can fail with a lot of education, too. I'm not saying [education] is the only way to do it, but I think that this is the best way to do it. It gives you a lot to fall back on." Running a commercial brewery means running the finances, production, and distribution of beer at a large scale, something a homebrewer might find difficult to master without professional exposure and experience.

Education is about more than knowing the right mineral content for your brewing water or being aware of which hops lend well to certain flavor profiles. Schoneman says, "It's not necessarily [knowing] what to do; it's what to do when something goes wrong." Mistakes will be made, and some part of the brewing process will surely not go according to plan. But those mistakes and hiccups become apparent in beer quality and, according to Schoneman, "dumping a five- or ten-gallon batch is a lot different than dumping a 2,000-gallon batch."

The brewing profession is capital and labor intensive. The results of a mistake might not reveal themselves until the end of the brewing process, which may not leave a brewer with enough time (or money) to start over and rebrew the batch. As Schoneman explains, this puts brewers in a very difficult position. "If you're building a brewery and money's already super tight or you're completely out of money and it's time to sell beer, but you may have to dump it, that can break you right there. And I think there's probably several breweries that have gotten to that point, but not dumped that batch and sold it [instead]. And it's hurt them in the long run. Especially as more breweries come in to the brewing world, it's more critical than ever to really hit the ground running to make sure what you're doing right up front is really good, because the consumer is going to expect that as we go further down this road."

Both Schoneman and Wagner see brewing not as a glamorous hobby-turned-dream-job, but rather as a professional trade. This perspective falls in line with Schoneman's welding and tooling background. Steel Toe's brand even embraces the idea of brewing as a trade with its work boot logo and industrial taproom.

For the pair, it all comes down to working hard to produce something great. "Beer quality is just so important to us," Schoneman emphasizes. While that may not seem like a particularly revolutionary concept, Wagner says he sees that attitude lacking in the industry as a whole: "It's because the balance is shifted further and further away from getting education and experience [first] and *then* opening a brewery or working toward opening a brewery." Steel Toe aims to

Steel Toe's industrial suburban taproom is often filled with regulars.

tip the balance back in favor of technically excellent beer rooted in knowledge and experience.

Schoneman and Wagner work to impart that same knowledge to the taproom staff at Steel Toe, who are expected to be well versed not only in the company's brewing tactics but in the industry as a whole. The staff of fifteen—which Wagner estimates to be about a third to half the size of that at other breweries with comparable production—mostly came to Steel Toe with significant industry experience. Plus, when a new employee starts with Steel Toe, they are inducted into the company with a day in the brewhouse, which Schoneman refers to as "beer school." Schoneman and Wagner want to be sure that the people who work for them and serve their beers are well informed about the products and the process, since the owner and brewer are not there to explain to customers every pint that Steel Toe pours.

The customers at Steel Toe definitely notice the quality produced by a dedicated, educated staff. Perhaps it's simply loyalty to their local watering hole, but the fact that a brewery has a set of devoted regulars can be a fair measure of the brewery's commitment to quality. Schoneman says of the Steel Toe customers, "They're very honest and open with us."

Wagner adds that the craft beer consumer as a demographic in Minnesota is relatively young. They are educated enough to like craft beer, but with Minnesota's industry being newer than those in Oregon, Colorado, or California, the consumers still have a ways to go. Information that breweries in other states might take for granted in their customers must be introduced to the general consciousness here in Minnesota.

BREWING PHILOSOPHIES

Steel Toe's brewing philosophy originates with balance and drinkability. "Beer is supposed to be very drinkable," Wagner says. "Whether you're talking about English pub culture or German beer hall culture, the tradition of drinking beer is that it's a social thing. There is some aspect to the American craft beer culture where people crave these things that are these 'white whales' of very high value, but that's not really what beer is." He adds that beer should be balanced and approachable because "it's the everyday man's drink."

Just as it is with the brewery's blue-collar branding, Steel Toe's beer is focused on the average working American. Schoneman describes it simply: "What we focus on is just approachable, super high-quality, simple yet interesting beers."

Still, Wagner explains that, while Steel Toe focuses on brewing classic, drinkable beers, it also must keep an eye on market trends. So Steel Toe walks the line between balanced drinkability and hyped-up, flavor-extreme recipes. They'll never be a hype brewery, churning out "white whales," but they are responsive to the consumer.

One reason Steel Toe can afford to ignore some of the hype is its growth model. As a brewery "with big dreams of staying small," Steel Toe isn't chasing production volume increases. It's a tough balance to strike—a brewer can't just make the styles of beer they prefer to drink like they could ten years ago—but Wagner and Schoneman are holding on to their integrity tightly. This is evident in their products.

BEERS TO KNOW

Provider Ale: "Brewed to be light and refreshing with a slightly sweet bready malt flavor and floral hop aroma. Unfiltered to bring out the subtle yeast flavors. Hints of lemon peel and honey biscuit in both aroma and flavor." 5% ABV, 15 IBU

Dissent Dark Ale: "Bold and complex from a tremendous amount of roasted malts, with a rich, velvety mouthfeel from the addition of oats. Dissent has its own opinion of what a dark beer should be. Bittersweet dark chocolate, hints of coffee, and malted cream." 7% ABV, 50 IBU

Size 4 Session IPA: "Brewed to embody the best hop qualities of a highly aromatic and flavorful IPA, yet ever mindful of the desire to have a few. Loaded with pungent hops to impart aromas of blueberry, lime candy, and juicy fruit; a defined yet balanced bitterness finishes the beer." 4.5% ABV, 44 IBU

Size 7 IPA: "We take prodigious amounts of hops and add them any chance we get to this Pacific Northwest–style IPA. Big aroma and flavor of zesty orange peel, a dry and clean bitterness finishes in the most satisfying way possible." 7% ABV, 77 IBU

Wee Heavy Scotch Ale: "A traditional Scotch-style wee heavy strong ale, built with a backbone of traditional UK malt. Aromas and flavor present are big rich caramel, hints of graham cracker, and dark pit fruit. The body is full and luxurious. Low to moderate earthy hops are only there to balance. Slight pleasantly warming finish." 9.5% ABV

Before the Dawn Barrel-Aged Barleywine: "An American black barleywine aged in rye whiskey barrels. The aroma of whiskey, toasted marshmallow, dark chocolate, and subtle dark fruit prevail. The flavor matches the aroma, with a warming boozy yet pleasant finish. Big oak and drying tannins help to finish and balance the sweetness up front." 12% ABV

TOE

STEEL TOE
USA
ST. LOUIS PARK,
SIZE
INDIA PALE
12 FL OZ

Lunker Barrel-Aged Barleywine: "An English-style barleywine aged in rye whiskey barrels. Rye whiskey aromas followed by caramel, toffee, vanilla, oak char, and toasted bread notes. The rich, full-bodied character and sweetness of Lunker is tempered by the moderate bitterness." 13.5% ABV

AWARDS TO KNOW

2013 North American Beer Awards: Lunker, Silver Medal, Barrel-aged Strong Beer category

2014 Great American Beer Festival: Wee Heavy, Gold Medal, Scotch Ale category

2014 North American Beer Awards: Rainmaker Double Red Ale, Silver Medal, Double/Imperial Red Ale category

2014 North American Beer Awards: Size 4, Bronze Medal, American-style Pale Ale category

2014 World Beer Cup: Wee Heavy, Gold Medal, Scotch Ale category

2015 Great American Beer Festival: Size 4, Silver Medal, Session India Pale Ale category

2015 North American Beer Awards: Dissent, Silver Medal, Foreign-style Stout category

2015 North American Beer Awards: Provider, Bronze Medal, English-style Summer Ale category

2015 North American Beer Awards: Wee Heavy, Bronze Medal, Scotch Ale category

2018 Great American Beer Festival: Dissent, Gold Medal, Export Stout category

2018 Great American Beer Festival: Provider, Silver Medal, English-style Summer Ale category

2018 World Beer Cup: Provider, Silver Medal, English-Style Summer Ale category

Size 7 IPA is a hoppy, Pacific Northwest–style brew.

PORTAGE BREWING COMPANY

A STORY OF RESILIENCE, COMMUNITY, AND CRAFT IN OUTSTATE MINNESOTA

Walker, Minnesota

Opened: April 2017; reopened December 2019

Barrels produced (2018): 306; 107th largest in state by production

Barrels produced (2019, partial year): 122

The Team: Jeff Vondenkamp, co-owner and head brewer

Rob Braswell, lead brewer

Danielle DeVille, marketing

AROUND THE WORLD AND BACK AGAIN

Jeff Vondenkamp first fell in love with beer while traveling abroad. When he was twenty-eight years old, he quit his job at the Lyft company headquarters in San Francisco for what he called "cultural exploration." In places like Nepal and Vietnam, Vondenkamp saw how craft reflected communities and brought together expats and locals. In 2016, he wrote an article for *The Growler* called "Culture in a Glass: Lessons Learned Drinking through South Asia," in which he shared his experiences from his world travels. "You can learn a lot by being curious and thirsty," he wrote. "Wherever I was unable to speak or understand, we simply drank, smiled, or high-fived. Technology makes it easy to forego real human conversations and experiences. Resist. Put your phone in your pocket, look up, and take a left. The flavors and friendliness that will be granted to you from those you encounter will humble you and subdue your fears for good."

In an interview with that same magazine just over a year later—during which time Vondenkamp had opened his Portage Brewing Company in Walker, Minnesota—he again reflected on the transformational experience of his travels. "It changed my perspective on almost every philosophical issue, but a big one was the connection to local community and craft that I'd seen a lot of abroad. Many people

Co-owner and head brewer Jeff Vondenkamp checks in on Portage's expanded barrel program, a sizeable passion project of his.

over there have never left the small villages in which they were born. They have a task that helps their community survive. That's it. The simplest form of commerce and connection you can have."

Vondenkamp was exploring Nepal with no plans to return to Minnesota—much less the town of Walker—when he got a call from his dad. The elder Vondenkamp asked his son, "Would you ever consider moving back and opening a brewery here in Walker?"

The answer was a resounding no. Vondenkamp went on to three more weeks of trekking with no cell service. After consideration and reflection, however, Vondenkamp began to warm to the idea of building a brewery with his family in the town where they had owned a cabin for many years.

He realized he was driven to create something that he could hand to a customer and watch them experience it. The intangibility of his work at Lyft left him looking for more. That's why he had started homebrewing back in 2009, and perhaps it's also why he latched on to the craft beer scene in his travels—the product offered a lens through which to view the social and cultural forces around him.

Upon his return stateside, Vondenkamp got to work opening a brewery with his parents. The brewery launched in April 2017, a few weeks before the fishing opener and just in time for cabin season. The market for beer in the town of fewer than a thousand year-round residents was sufficient to support a brewery throughout the year, and it skyrocketed in summers, with cabin-goers flocking to town to visit Leech Lake or one of the dozen-plus other lakes within easy driving distance.

Vondenkamp and the team brought on Rob Braswell, a Walker local, in July 2017. Braswell had gotten out of Dodge after his junior year of college and moved to Portland, where he lived for five years. When Braswell came back to town, he was hanging out at a local haunt when he heard about a new brewery in town, called Portage. He applied for a job there and was quickly hired on as a bartender. He worked his way up to cellarman and eventually became the lead brewer. He now works side by side with Vondenkamp in the brewhouse, and he has even developed his own recipes.

Portage Brewing built its reputation on rotating beers and funky fermentations; the Coffeecake Ale was a crowd favorite from the beginning, and the brewery has been recognized for its wild sour program. The brewers also "strive to push the limits of ingredient flavor and aroma in the IPA style," says Vondenkamp. "For years, we've been tinkering on what we're finding among the more complex styles. We usually have one to three of these styles on at a time, and will continue to seek the limits of new hop and barley varieties out there." As a brewery known for small-batch experimental brewing, the brewers' interests are always prioritized. The styles they brew shift with the seasons and their curiosities.

In addition to its creative and fluid approach to its beer styles, Portage was also one of few places in the area that served as an inclusive hangout for all types of people. That made it all the more tragic when, nine months after opening, the historic building that housed Portage Brewing burned to the ground in the wee hours of January 6, 2018.

RISING FROM THE ASHES

On the evening of Saturday, January 5, a group of local volunteer firefighters celebrated a colleague's fiftieth birthday in the taproom. Little did they know, just hours later they would be back at the brewery to put out the flames that engulfed it. Among those firefighters was Joe Arndt, a co-owner of the brewery. The source of the fire was never confirmed, and the eighty-eight-year-old building—once the town hospital—wasn't up to modern safety standards.

In a letter published in *The Growler* in December 2019, Vondenkamp described that January day and the weeks that followed as "some of the hardest for our family and team. This place—where we spent thousands of hours caring, creating, and communing with people we care about, over a product we're all so passionate about—gone, cast out into the cold Minnesota air."

Portage had become a gathering space for the community in the short time it was open. When hit with the devastating news of the fire, its patrons quickly responded. That weekend, community members held a benefit for Portage at the local event center. Coincidentally, Portage had been planning to release its Resilience IPA that night, part of an international collaboration coordinated by Sierra Nevada to raise funds for the victims of the Camp Fire in California. The same volunteer firefighters who had quelled the blaze at Portage less than a week earlier were pouring the beer that evening, bringing even deeper meaning to the event for the Walker community.

As devastating as the fire was to the team and the community, the Portage crew did not hesitate in their decision to rebuild. Brewer Rob Braswell took a call from Vondenkamp while he was on a catamaran in Hawaii. Vondenkamp asked Braswell, "Do you want to keep going? Because we are going to keep going." Braswell was on board, without question.

Rather than dwelling on the loss of their taproom, their beer, and a staple of the community, the Portage team took the fire as an opportunity to improve on what they had before. Danielle DeVille, who handles marketing for Portage, says, "the fire gave us a chance to rebuild the brewery we always envisioned." While they could not replace the history of the building itself, they could build a space that functioned even better to serve their community.

With the rebuild, which was completed in early December 2019, Portage expanded its square footage by 30 percent, doubled the brewing system and increased production capacity by 45 percent, and tripled the cellaring space. While the brewery was being rebuilt, Braswell worked at Back Channel Brewing on Lake Minnetonka and gained additional commercial experience. The team also rereleased a collaboration beer with their friends at Modist Brewing in Minneapolis. Jackson Greer, now the head brewer at Modist, is a Walker local and had become friends with the Portage team. Modist donated 100 percent of the sales—not just the profits—to Portage's rebuild. Other Minnesota breweries, such as BlackStack in St. Paul, also kept Portage brewing with collaboration releases and offered other forms of support.

In addition to expanding the square footage and brewing capacity, the Portage team built the new taproom to function better as a community space. The walls and support beams that were structurally integral to the original building limited the use of the space, so they opted for an open concept in the new taproom. It includes different types of seating to accommodate large groups, intimate date nights, and individuals looking for a quiet corner. Plus, the massively expanded patio is perfect for summertime drinking.

Today, Vondenkamp sees his work at the brewery as a convergence of the different experiences from his twenties. At Portage, he brings together his branding experience from Lyft, his appreciation for community from traveling, and his love of the outdoors. The brewery allows Vondenkamp to do things like collect wild yeast from the Chippewa National Forest just beyond the brewery's backyard while expanding Portage Brewing Company with creative beer recipes that reflect his interests and values, design, and a larger vision for the brand

Before a devastating fire destroyed the original taproom, Portage was a popular gathering space for humans and dogs alike.

Portage opened a swanky new taproom in December 2019, less than two years after a fire destroyed the original brewery and taproom. *Photo by Sam Ziegler*

as a whole. His hands-on work is responsible for building a brand, a community center, and some damn good beer.

BEERS TO KNOW

Coffeecake Blonde Ale: "Our very first and most popular recipe at Portage, brewed to mimic a piece of fluffy coffee cake. We use our house Portage Coffee, Ceylon cinnamon, and vanilla beans to achieve those notes. Beneath that, though, we've built a grain bill that expresses lots of caramel and biscuit flavors." 5.2% ABV, 18 IBU

Chatter Chatter Czech Pils: "The most frequently drunk beer of our brewing staff. Made with crushability as the centerpiece while respecting the tradition of this style. German floor malted malts, Czech Saaz hops, and a famous pilsner yeast strain. Simple and bright." 5.2% ABV, 30 IBU

ABLOOM: "Our head brewer's baby and his most passionate style of brewing. From the cultivation of spontaneous yeast from berry and flowers in pollination, we grab these hosts and bring them into our process. From mixed fermentation saisons, to gueuze, to hybrid ale styles, we'll continue pushing the limits of craft beer through this program. All of these beers are also oak fermented and aged before package conditioning."

A tasty sample of one of the first beers released in the new Portage taproom.

THE FUTURE OF CRAFT BEER

Craft beer has boomed. Now, it's maintaining. Or, it was maintaining until 2020. The effects of the COVID-19 pandemic on craft breweries and other businesses are yet to be fully realized by the time this book goes to press. The year began with plans for beer festivals, anniversary parties, and summers full of new beer releases. One by one, these events were canceled due to the dangers of COVID. As I write this, the brewery I work for is planning for its second major business-model change in three months in response to the economic challenges brought about by the "stay at home" order and the closure of many businesses throughout the spring of 2020. Collectively and individually, the brewing industry is scrambling to cobble together new delivery programs, secure government loans, and develop beer-to-go programs to help mitigate the losses from taproom closures. Sales teams are mourning the near-total dearth of bar and restaurant business and meanwhile are struggling to meet the increased demand at liquor stores, most of which remained open while the rest of the retail economy largely slowed to a crawl.

Stocks of crowler cans are running dangerously low thanks to robust beer-to-go sales that no one was prepared for; crowler suppliers are either rationing inventory or turning away business altogether. This is a result of the massive increase in demand for the 750-milliliter (25.4-ounce) cans, but the shortage is also due to the fact that Minnesota is one of few states to use this size of crowler. Most other states sell 32-ounce crowlers, so production companies are responding to that demand first. And even though many breweries have their own canning lines and could supply customers with canned beer, legal restrictions prohibit Minnesota taprooms from selling beer in 12- and 16-ounce vessels from out their own doors. The Minnesota Craft Brewers Guild and other independent craft-beer advocates lobbied the Minnesota state legislature to allow a temporary lift on the ban of four- and six-pack sales in taprooms. The #freethefourpack initiative eventually failed, however, due to the stubbornness and influence of the liquor coalition and the unwillingness of legislators to stand up for small businesses in their districts.

According to the Brewers Association, regional craft brewers were static in 2018, and most breweries produced the same volume as they did in previous years. But the continued opening of new breweries and growth within the microbrewery category have contributed to the craft segment's overall growth prior to the COVID economy. Interestingly, microbreweries contributed 80 percent of the craft category's total growth in 2018, up from 60 percent in 2017. Put simply, this means American craft beer growth is coming from new breweries, not an increase in volume from our largest craft brewers. With this increase in the number of breweries, we have also seen an increase in taproom sales overall. Bart Watson, chief economist for the Brewers Association, noted in 2019 that the taproom model was booming nationally, but while visitor count is increasing, the rate of new patrons isn't keeping up with the rate of brewery openings. Watson says, "Craft has settled into a more mature growth pattern and is unlikely to return to the meteoric growth levels seen over the past decade."

We're seeing these trends here in Minnesota, too. Of our three largest brewers (Summit, Surly, and Schell's), Schell's has been declining in production for three years and Surly for two. Summit suffered a big dip in production in 2017 but increased annual production in the years following, eventually leveling back up to their pre-dip numbers in 2019. Our other five craft regional brands (Fulton Brewing, Castle Danger Brewery, Third Street Brewhouse, Indeed Brewing, and Bent Paddle Brewing)—defined by the Brewers Association as producing more than 15,000 barrels—are a mixed bag as well. Indeed and Bent Paddle saw decreased production in the last year, Castle Danger and Third Street increased, and Fulton remained flat.

Sure, we might not have the next Sam Adams on our hands, in terms of level of growth, but Minnesota is home to Fair State Brewing Cooperative, which exploded from producing 1,300 barrels to nearly 19,000 barrels over the course of just five years. Today the state has more than 170 taproom-based microbreweries, up from 90 in 2015.

In his analysis of the industry in April 2019, Bart Watson of the Brewers Association observed that whether the craft beer market has reached equilibrium or is continuing to grow is largely a factor of geography and business model. "If you're a widely distributed production brewery in Portland, Denver, or San Diego, you probably see a pretty mature market. If you're a taproom brewer in Birmingham, Little Rock, or Lexington, you probably see more run room."

Minnesota falls more into the second category, as the industry continues to see opportunity for growth. Twenty-five new breweries opened in the state in 2019. Two of those were located in Minneapolis, a trio found homes in the Twin Cities suburbs, and the remainder represent small towns and metropolitan areas in outstate Minnesota. Nine of the new breweries in 2019 were brewpubs, which blows previous years' numbers out of the water (only six brewpubs opened in 2017 and 2018 combined).

Brian Kaufenberg, editor of *The Growler* magazine, wrote in November 2019, "In the past two years, flat and negative growth at the regional brewery level has quashed any dreams a brewery may have of starting the next Sierra Nevada. Instead, the trend is toward opening taprooms that operate more as neighborhood pubs (where the profit margin of a pint is significantly better than the retail market)." He also predicts a growth in the production and proliferation of hard seltzer and breweries expanding to locations outside of Minnesota, just as Lupulin and Indeed have done.

Lauren Bennett McGinty, executive director of the Minnesota Craft Brewers Guild, calls on the example of Spiral Brewery in Hastings to

BREWERY OPENINGS AND CLOSINGS

NATIONWIDE, BY YEAR

2015: 921 opened, 105 closed

2016: 1,080 opened, 120 closed

2017: 1,198 opened, 202 closed

2018: 1,121 opened, 242 closed

2019: 942 opened, 294 closed

illustrate how breweries will continue to open in and revitalize small towns. While she predicts that we will see some breweries close in the next five years, she also believes that small-town taprooms are the new corner pub. She says of Spiral Brewery: "They opened up on the main street in downtown Hastings, and within the year they were insanely, wildly popular. The main street itself started growing, and they started adding more shops, and other shops would redo their outside or freshen up their look. ... I just loved that concept of young people going back to their hometowns and helping contribute to the place where they grew up and hopefully drawing in more people."

As Minnesota brewers are fulfilling new niches, opening up as neighborhood pubs rather than production breweries, they are also fulfilling consumer demands with the styles they produce. Craft brewers are pushing the boundaries of what we traditionally think of as beer and simultaneously attempting to guide consumers back toward traditional recipes. The same brewery that is known for hazy IPAs or pastry stouts will also proudly produce a classic pilsner, and the brewers themselves are often drinking those very lagers when they reach for a beer.

NEW BREWERIES/BREWPUBS OPENED IN MINNESOTA

BY YEAR

2013: 15
2014: 24
2015: 25
2016: 19
2017: 34
2018: 28
2019: 25

Brewers are constantly balancing the demands of consumer preferences against their own desires to guide the market in the directions they want it to go. For example, some breweries jumped on the hard seltzer train early, while others refuse to touch the beverage. But the same brewer who won't produce a seltzer might also release a triple-adjunct pastry stout—illustrating that each brewer has their own ideas about what are appropriate divergences from so-called traditional brewing. August Schell Brewing, for example, produces the classic Grain Belt premium lager while also selling the trend-feeding Sangria citrus lager.

Some Minnesota brewers push the envelope through experimentation within tradition, such as wild fermentation, barrel aging and fermenting, or using new varieties of yeast to speed up production time. Others focus on the source of their ingredients, working with local organic farmers for adjuncts or highlighting Minnesota-grown hops. Where some brewers construct carefully balanced tap lists or brands, others unapologetically lean into their niche styles.

The goal here is not to nitpick each business's strategies and philosophies in order to distill the Minnesota craft beer industry down to a singular, ideal brewery. Instead, I want to acknowledge and encourage a diverse market where there is a brewery for every drinker and mood, a culture where brewers may learn from one another as they push their personal boundaries of craftsmanship, and an attitude that welcomes experts and novices alike into the wonderful world of craft beer.

RECOMMENDED READING

Sometimes it seems like there are nearly as many books about beer as there are beers to drink. Whether you want cookbooks and cocktail recipes or chemistry-driven style descriptions, there is a book for you. I've selected a few books and magazines that were foundational to my own knowledge of beer and the craft beer industry. I could recommend hundreds of other books written by industry professionals and observers alike, but these are a great place to start.

Doug Hoverson, *Land of Amber Waters: The History of Brewing in Minnesota* (2007) and *The Drink That Made Wisconsin Famous: Beer and Brewing in the Badger State* (2019)

Doug Hoverson, a Minnesota native and author of this book's foreword, details an enormous history of beer and brewing in Minnesota and Wisconsin.

Steve Hindy, *The Craft Beer Revolution: How a Band of Microbrewers Is Transforming the World's Favorite Drink* (2014)

If beer geek history interests you, I highly recommend Steve Hindy's book. Hindy, cofounder of Brooklyn Brewery, tells the inside story of how a band of entrepreneurial homebrewers and microbrewers built the craft beer industry and challenged the dominance of the national beer brands and the way Americans look at beer.

Garrett Oliver, *The Brewmaster's Table: Discovering the Pleasures of Real Beer with Real Food* (2005)

Garrett Oliver, Steve Hindy's partner at the influential Brooklyn Brewery, explores the wide range of flavors in beer and how the beverage makes a perfect companion to food.

Beer for two at the Finnegans bar.

Michael Jackson, *The World Guide to Beer* (1977), *Michael Jackson's Beer Companion* (1997), and many more

Michael Jackson's books provide important insights into beer styles, and he is considered the godfather of beer critics.

The Growler magazine

Now shuttered, *The Growler* was a free, monthly publication that covered Minnesota's beer, drink, and food communities, celebrating the "craft lifestyle." Founded in 2012, it offered resources, reviews, and analysis of beer and "all things craft." It was owned by the Beer Dabbler, which hosts three popular annual beer festivals. I still recommend picking up old issues or reading through articles online.

The New Brewer magazine

The New Brewer is the journal of the Brewers Association, a trade organization for the American brewing industry, with a particular focus on craft beer and homebrewing. First published in 1983, the magazine offers practical insights and advice for craft breweries of all sizes, including information on brewing technology, business management, sales and marketing, raw materials, beer styles, industry news, and more.

SELECTED SOURCES

American Homebrewers Association, "United States Sees Historic Number of Breweries." Homebrewersassociation.org, December 2, 2015.

Bland, Alastair. "After a Long Day of Fighting Climate Change, This Grain Is Ready for a Beer." National Public Radio, October 26, 2016.

Brandt, Steve. "City Council Could Open Doors for Brewers." *Minneapolis Star Tribune*, August 2, 2010.

Brewers Association. "2020 Brewers Association Beer Style Guidelines." Brewersassociation.org.

———. "Minnesota's Craft Beer Sales & Production Statistics, 2019." Brewersassociation.org.

———. "National Beer Sales & Production Data." *The New Brewer* (May/June 2019).

Collins, John. "Surly Brewing Finally Taps into the Law It Helped Create." Minnesota Public Radio News, October 29, 2013.

Fagerberg, Jerard. "Minnesota Breweries Are Coming to Disrupt the $500 Million Hard Seltzer Market." *City Pages*, February 13, 2019.

Farniok, Ben. "North Shore Town Bans Bent Paddle Beer Over PolyMet Fight." *Minneapolis Star Tribune*, March 15, 2016.

Great American Beer Festival. "FAQ: Attendees." Greatamericanbeerfestival.com.

Green, Loren. "The Increasingly Blurry Line Between Brewpubs and Breweries." *The Growler*, January 21, 2016.

Hindy, Steve. "Free Craft Beer!" *New York Times*, March 29, 2014.

Horgen, Tom. "Brewing Comes Home." *Minneapolis Star Tribune*, February 8, 2011.

Jackson, Sharyn. "New Minnesota Breweries Bring Diversity: 'Beer Is the Ultimate Cross-Cultural Thing.'" *Minneapolis Star Tribune*, November 24, 2018.

Kaufenberg, Brian. "2019 Year in Review: Beer, Cider, and ... Seltzer." *The Growler*, November 26, 2019.

Kendall, Justin. "Beer Market Share Falls Below 50 Percent in 2018." Brewbound.com, April 4, 2019.

Livingston-Garcia, Louis. "Where the Wild Beers Are: More Minnesota Brewers Are Investing in Mixed-Culture Programs." *The Growler*, July 17, 2019.

Lovgren, Andrew. "Toast to the North: Dabbling in the Great Outdoors." *The Growler*, January 31, 2017.

Mason, Joshua, and John Remakel. "Brew Pub v. Taproom: Which Business Model Is Right for You?" *Bar Examiner* (Summer 2015).

McCulla, Theresa. "Prohibition Was Fantastic for American Beer, or, Cheers to Homebrewers." *O Say Can You See: Stories from the Museum*, National Museum of American History, April 7, 2018.

McCullough, Michael, Joshua Berning, and Jason L. Hanson. "Learning by Brewing: Homebrewing Legalization and the Brewing Industry." *Contemporary Economic Policy*, May 31, 2018.

Minnesota Legislature. Bill H.F. No. 1326. May 24, 2011. www.revisor.mn.gov/laws/2011/0/Session+Law/Chapter/55/.

O'Brien, Jeffrey. "Can Law Changes Help Avoid a Minnesota Craft Beer 'Bubble'?" Jeffrey O'Brien Today, July 7, 2015.

Oldenburg, Ray. *The Great Good Place*. 3rd ed. New York: Marlowe & Company, 1999.

Renalls, Candace. "Stalled Brewpub Bill Stymies Fitger's Brewhouse Distribution Plan." *Duluth News Tribune*, June 20, 2011.

Roper, Eric. "Minneapolis Explores Easing Church-Spirits Separation." *Minneapolis Star Tribune*, November 6, 2011.

Sanchez, Gabriel. "Fair State Brewing Bringing Co-Op Model to New St. Paul HQ." *St. Paul Pioneer Press*, September 29, 2016.

Walsh, Paul. "Minneapolis Taproom Says It Is First to Win OK to Allow Dogs Indoors." *Minneapolis Star Tribune*, May 30, 2017.

Watson, Bart. "Craft Drinkers by DMA and Gender." Brewers Association, June 12, 2018.

———. "The Demographics of Craft Beer Lovers." Brewers Association, 2014.

White, Rebekah. "A Third Place." *New Zealand Geographic* (July-August 2018).

INDEX

Page numbers in *italics* indicate illustrations.